SEVEN

The Number for Happiness, Love, and Success

Jacqueline Leo

TWELVE

NEW YORK • BOSTON

Twelve
Hachette Book Group
237 Park Avenue
New York, NY 10017

www.HachetteBookGroup.com

Twelve is an imprint of Grand Central Publishing.
The Twelve name and logo are trademarks of Hachette Book Group, Inc.

Printed in the United States of America

First Edition: December 2009

10 9 8 7 6 5 4 3 2 1

Library of Congress Cataloging-in-Publication Data

Leo, Jacqueline.
    Seven : the number for happiness, love, and success /
Jacqueline Leo.—1st ed.
        p. cm.
    Includes index.
    ISBN 978-0-446-54269-2
    1. Happiness. 2. Love. 3. Success. 4. Numerology. I. Title.
    BF575.H27L455 2009
    158—dc22
                                                            2009012075

Book design by Douglas Turshen

{ FOR JOHN }

All human actions have one or more of
these seven causes: chance, nature,
compulsion, habit, reason, passion, and desire.
—Aristotle (384 B.C.–322 B.C.)

Contents

I've Got Your Number

A few years ago, when I was editing *Family Circle* magazine, we decided to publish a classic cookbook. The magazine was well known for its triple-tested recipes but had never taken that giant step into the world of trade book publishing to compete with the hundreds of other cookbooks on the shelves: books by Julia Child, *Better Homes and Gardens*, *Gourmet* magazine, and others. Many of these "food bibles" offered 1,000 recipes or more. But as I sifted through the data and delved into the research, I learned something even more interesting. People who purchased these cookbooks used, on average, about 7 out of the 1,000 recipes available. Why so few?

I talked to a few friends and associates about this seeming anomaly and became even more intrigued when one said, "Doesn't surprise me. I have a closet stuffed with clothes, yet I always seem to wear the same seven outfits each week." One man told me that he couldn't deal with the choices at the coffee shop near his office, so he ordered the daily special regardless of what was offered.

George Miller, a Harvard University psychology professor in the 1950s, was also intrigued with the number seven. While his

colleague B. F. Skinner was working on advances in behavioral psychology, Miller focused on cognitive science. He published his landmark study, "The Magical Number Seven, Plus or Minus Two: Some Limits on Our Capacity for Processing Information," in the *Psychological Review* in 1956. He opens with this thought: "My problem is that I have been persecuted by an integer. For seven years this number has followed me around, has intruded in my most private data, and has assaulted me from the pages of our most public journals."

Miller completed a series of measurements, experiments, and data and showed the limits of the human mind to remember large amounts of information. He established that the average person can hold up to seven numbers, words, or visual objects in short-term or working memory. (Some say that telephone numbers were limited to seven digits because of this finding.)

Seven is a natural brain filter, managing information and visual stimuli in order to let the brain and memory function properly. What Miller couldn't anticipate was the overwhelming amount of information and electronic stimulation that would result from computing and the Internet. But that overload is rewiring our brains and causing us to flit from reading an e-mail, to listening to our iPods, to making a cell phone call, to reading a tweet, to watching a video. It's mental hopscotching, and young and old are now both victims of memory impairment.

My twenty-six-year-old daughter is an editor at a popular political website. She has always loved books, and had started a book club after graduating from college. A few months ago, she confided that she had lost her ability to read long passages in the novel she had selected without taking a break or doing something else. She decided to retrain her brain by forcing herself to read without any interruptions. It took a few months, but she's back in her groove. I wondered how many others her age were similarly affected by the digital noise in their everyday lives. I decided to create a simple "memory survey" and give it to two groups: ages 22–30, and ages 45–65. Here's what I found:

STATEMENT	YOUNG	OLD
I forget appointments.	41%	45%
I forget people's names immediately after they have introduced themselves.	82%	87%
I find I cannot remember something that is on the tip of my tongue.	29%	35%
I forget important dates like birthdays and anniversaries.	41%	45%
Even though I put things in a special place, I still forget where they are.	53%	51%
I find that I have read several paragraphs without being able to recall what I read.	59%	48%
I have gone into a room to get something, gotten distracted, and left without what I went there for.	76%	80%
I begin one task and get distracted into doing something else.	76%	69%
I have to go back to check whether I have done something or not (e.g., turning out the lights, locking doors).	76%	78%
I make mistakes because I am doing one thing and thinking about another.	59%	43%

George Miller's theory might explain why we should use the number seven to clean up the pollution in our brains and regain some cognitive control. But what about the other phenomena? What about the Seven Wonders of the World, the seven seas, the seven ages of man, the seven daughters of Atlas in the Pleiades, the seven levels of hell, the seven primary colors, the seven notes of the musical scale, and the seven days of the week? Why were there only "7 Habits of Highly Effective People"? Why only seven dwarfs, seven ingredients in a Big Mac, seven continents? Why were there originally only seven deadly sins (lust, greed, pride, wrath, sloth, envy, gluttony), especially since it's so easy to think of at least a dozen more?

Why were the Seven Sisters a group of women's colleges, a group of Stalinist skyscrapers in Moscow, and a group of popular magazines aimed at women? And why, when asked to choose a number between 1 and 10, do most people choose 7? Why is there a seven-year-itch and why do the opposite sides of a die add up to seven? I began to investigate why the number seven played such a dominant role in religion, science, the arts, literature, business, and education.

Seven can not only filter the flood of information that constantly assaults us in our daily lives, it can also help us make smart choices when we search for a job, purchase a house, or even shop for orange juice. Seven can help us find the right words at the right time, and avoid the words and phrases that undermine or embarrass us. I learned that the number seven is that near-perfect value, and I wanted to celebrate and share its wonderful and ancient history. I also discovered that seven has been used as a tool to define time, synthesize ideas, and keep one's mind and memory performing at top speed. Seven shows us how to get the most out of life and give the best of ourselves. It makes everyday living a little bit better.

SCALLOP'S EDGE

Cena della Vigilia, the Feast of the Seven Fishes, is an Italian Christmas tradition. The meal commemorates the wait of the birth of the baby Jesus. The decorative shell is also a symbol of fertility.
—Sources: Saveur.com; Wikipedia

CHAPTER 1

Simplicity

Nothing is enough for the man to whom enough is too little.
—Epicurus

Why do we group so many things in sevens? Seven is more than a lucky number or a famous baseball player's uniform. It's the brain's natural shepherd, herding vast amounts of information into manageable chunks. It's also a special tool that can help you make smart decisions and sift through all the choices of modern life. Even more important, seven can filter the digital static that comes from being connected to our cell phones, iPods, e-mail, TV, and the Internet. This useful digit can help disentangle a complicated life, leaving time for real work, family, and friends. Seven keeps it simple.

When life got easier, it got harder. We used to wait in line at the bank to deposit or withdraw cash. We had to walk down streets to search for an empty telephone booth. We had to wrench ourselves out of an easy chair to change the dial on a console TV from one of the three broadcast networks to another. There was a dearth of catalogs, and no Internet, so shopping meant going to a store. We had to rely on one or two guidance counselors to give sage advice to hundreds of anxious high school seniors who hoped to get into college.

Technology made these tasks easier, but not without serious costs. Automated teller machines (ATMs) brought great convenience, but also more muggings, the first of many confusing PIN numbers, and identity theft. The walk-to public telephone booth was replaced by the cell phone; the remote control gave birth to the couch potato; and mall walking, the calisthenics of the credit card set, had to compete with desktop shopping. The less we walk, the more weight we gain. The more weight we gain, the greater the incidence of type 2 diabetes. And, at many high schools, guidance counselors have been replaced by virtual campus tours and online applications.

We are living in an on-demand world, where information, acquisition, and personal contact are instant and ubiquitous. And that means that most of us, along with our social networks— family, friends, colleagues, merchants, and others—have overloaded our brains with daily stimuli.

Do, Re, Mi . . .

There are seven whole notes in an octave.

I would not want to eliminate or change any of the advances that have been made in the past fifty years (especially the E-Z Pass). But all this change is messing with our bodies and especially our minds. We have so many choices, so many interruptions, and so many distractions on any given day that our natural brain filters are forced into overdrive. These filters eliminate irrelevant information and allow us to focus on what's important. More often than not, that filter is the number seven. Aside from mythology, religion, and numerology, seven has been a practical tool for making things work and getting things done. We can hold on to seven: that's why the average workday is seven hours; why we can retain a seven-digit local telephone number; and why there are more than 835,000 books with the number seven in their titles, one of the most successful of which is Stephen Covey's *7 Habits of Highly Effective People*.

Before the tech revolution, people would daydream while waiting on line at the bank. They'd let their brains idle and recharge. They'd hum, whistle, or think while walking instead of talking on their cell phones or listening to their iPods. The word *stress* was barely part of the vocabulary. Life wasn't necessarily slower, but it was saner.

The next big leap of technology is about to change our lives yet again. It's the mobile Web, and it can invade your life in ways that will make you want to dive under the covers and stay there. The mobile Web uses technology that's been available outside of the U.S. for years called 3G, for "third generation." It turns a basic cell phone into a sophisticated high-speed Internet computer that enables messaging and social networking, Internet searches, downloads, electronic shopping, music, movies, and video games. The 3G iPhone from Apple has these features, and millions bought it as soon as it went on sale. Try sleeping on an airplane when they allow passengers to make phone calls. Try enjoying your favorite movie on your digital TV while advertisements crawl along the bottom of the flat screen like poisonous asps. Try getting into a taxi and telling the driver where you want to go over the voices of two local newscasters, on a split screen, telling you what you should have known before you left your house: that it's going to rain. For most of us, being "always on" means being always distracted, interrupted, and annoyed. Activating your brain's natural filter—consciously using seven to prioritize, organize, and limit the amount of stimuli you receive—can help you reclaim your focus, your balance, and even your life.

Ask people to pick a number from 1 to 10. The most popular choice will be 7. Some feel that seven is a safe number and choose it because it's above the mean but not at the top of the heap like ten. Others believe it's lucky or magical. I've learned that seven is useful and practical, a number that can help people effectively and efficiently cut through the clutter of life and hone in on the essentials. Consciously employing the number seven as a tool to accomplish goals and manage your life is not a new concept. After all, both God and Shakespeare thought enough of seven to use it in dramatic ways: God to create the Universe (we're including the day of rest, which no doubt was the inspiration for modern trade unions), and Shakespeare to identify the Seven Ages of Man: infant, schoolboy, lover, soldier, justice, pantaloon, and second childhood. (If Shakespeare had had the time or the inclination to identify the seven ages of woman, he might have suggested schoolgirl, scholar, lover, mother, careerist, divorcée, and silver fox.)

HOARDERS

We are a nation of hoarders. Not the obsessive-compulsive variety that results in piles of detritus and condemned houses. And not the over-the-top "I see it; I want it; I'll buy it" types. We just like to hold on to things. Of course, some of us can hoard more than others. After running one of the most corrupt governments of the twentieth century, Ferdinand Marcos, president of the Philippines, had pilfered enough money to let his wife, Imelda, buy anything she wanted. She didn't hold back. By the time she and her husband went into voluntary exile, she had amassed over 1,060 pairs of shoes.

Imelda Marcos broke at least two of the seven deadly sins: greed and gluttony. Why gluttony? Because hoarding is similar to overeating. When your body and brain are in sync, you know when to stop because a hormone called leptin is secreted by your fat cells and functions as an appetite suppressant. Leptin is to eating what the brain filter "seven" is to hoarding. Seven sets a limit and lets you know when you've had enough. There are only seven types of common women's shoes: boots, dress shoes, casual shoes, sandals, slides, flats, and athletic shoes. Of course within each category, there are many varieties. But even if one had enough closet space to store, say, seven

---

Magnificent Sevens

Two sports are played with teams of seven players:
team handball and water polo.

varieties of each, the total would be 49 pairs of shoes, not 1,060. The average person doesn't fly that high when it comes to hoarding. It's simply "I'll lose the weight and fit into those clothes again." Or "I'll need those papers someday."

Many of us have assigned a real value to our possessions and documents. We muse about making a killing on eBay, or magically extracting key data from those old floppy disks that will impress our bosses. But the real reason we keep too much stuff is because we have the space to do it—whether real or virtual. Since 1973 the average size of a single-family American home has increased almost 50 percent, from 1,660 square feet to 2,469 square feet in 2006. And that doesn't include the three-car garage or the basement.

Big homes, big cars, tiny office cubicles. But small work spaces mask our true virtual capacity. We have unlimited free space for our e-mails, photos, social networking sites, videos, blogs, music, games, and movies, with space left over for our files, bills, strategic reports, financial transactions, holiday lists, and miscellaneous documents. Moore's law, which states that the number of transistors on computer chips doubles every two years, has not only expanded our computing capacity; it's exploded it. Demand creates supply, which, in turn, creates new demand. So storage has become its own industry, from tiny thumb drives that can hold sixty-four gigabytes of data to the myriad outdoor and indoor physical facilities that are booming across the country. There's also a retail enterprise devoted solely to storage solutions called The Container Store where you can find hundreds of products to stylishly house your shoes, files, or even your garbage.

As a result, there's no need to throw things out, and so we keep it all: filing and archiving with the thought that every e-mail is as important as one of Lincoln's letters. Our egos tell us that everything we write is so brilliant that it must be saved for posterity. So we hoard and in the process, we overwhelm ourselves with "stuff." But here's the kicker: If and when we do want to dig something out, we can't find it. No matter how many color codes, file folders, customized icons, or other devices we use to get organized, it's almost impossible to keep up with the volume of e-mails and attachments that bombard us every day, as well as the news, professional updates, entertainment, phone calls, catalogs, magazines, text messages, and advertisements. We hoard because we can.

It's gotten so bad that an updated ascetic social movement has emerged during the past three decades called voluntary simplicity, in which disciples swear off consumerism in favor of more human contact and interaction. *Real Simple* magazine, with the tagline, "life made easier every day," poses the question: "Unless you've spent your adult life

---

Heads Up

In the opening scene of this thriller, all the building numbers start with 7. Brad Pitt, who played one of the detectives investigating a series of murders inspired by the seven deadly sins, earned millions for his role in the film. But Pitt didn't always have a big payday. In 1988 he was filming *The Dark Side of the Sun* in what was then Yugoslavia. His salary: $1,523 for seven weeks. The movie was almost complete when war broke out and the footage was lost. It took seven more years before the film was found. The movie was finally released in 1997.

pursuing some sort of monastic ideal, chances are you've had days when you felt buried by your possessions. You know—the clothes spilling from the drawers, the toys busting out of the baskets, the dishes overwhelming the cabinets. Where does it all come from?" Aside from Amazon, it probably comes from Costco, Wal-Mart, and Target, where the simple living movement is as terrifying to their executives as it is to the captains of Wall Street who know that it's the consumer that drives the U.S. economy.

Family structure also plays a role in how much stuff we acquire. When children of divorce celebrate Christmas, birthdays, Bar Mitzvahs, or graduations, they rake it in because of multiple sets of grandparents, cousins, aunts, uncles, etc. But the joy of toys can be lost when the bounty is greater than a child's ability to value it. How many stuffed animals does it take to become a "collection" rather than characters with names and personalities? When does the next action figure become a simple commodity instead of a genuine superhero? Even intact families can suffer from consumer overload. When my daughter Alexandra was three years old, she opened a present of six Nerf balls in a plastic tube. She emptied them out, sighed, and said, "Too many balls."

Simple living is a reaction to the unbridled acquisition of more and more stuff in both the real and virtual worlds. In the real world, your threads are the clothes stuffed into your closet. In the virtual world, threads are the endless e-mails that friends or colleagues send on a given subject, the longest of which is probably longer than the text in this book. E-mail is like atomic power: it can be both a blessing and a curse, depending on how it's used. At one company, the boss sent a message to her seven direct reports, saying that the company picnic would be held on June 21, and that before the event is announced to the entire staff, a meeting would take place to assign key planning tasks to managers. The categories: location options, food, games, music, entertainment, transportation, and budgeting. Seemed simple enough. But before one could say "Hold the mustard," the e-mails started flying. Instead of waiting for the meeting, the managers felt compelled to respond to their boss, and then to one another. It was a

---

World War 0

The Seven Years' War—the French and Indian War—(1756–63) never rose in the ranks of history compared to World Wars I and II, but because the major world powers at that time were involved, Sir Winston Churchill declared it the first true world war.

classic case of sycophantism laced with a healthy dose of in-house rivalry. The result was an e-mail thread, "re: picnic," that went on for fifty pages. So the boss pulled rank and instituted a new policy: "Any e-mail thread longer than 3 will be assigned to the dead pool. If there is anything left to say, get personal—talk to your co-workers directly, or, if necessary, schedule a meeting."

Professor John Maeda, who recently left MIT to head the Rhode Island School of Design, describes the first time his daughters got e-mail accounts in the first chapter of his book *The Laws of Simplicity.* "It began as a tiny drop...grew to a slow drip. Today it's a waterfall of messages, e-cards, and hyperlinks that showers upon them daily." He

---

&

None Too Many

Snow White probably could have found more, but she wisely
limited her social network to seven dwarfs.

confesses, "I find myself barely keeping afloat. I know that I'm not alone in this feeling of constantly drowning."

The psychological fallout of this overwhelming assault of information and acquisition is, among other things, stress. Stress caused by conflict. "Should I answer those last twenty e-mails or go home and play with my kids?" Stress can play diabolical tricks on your body and your mind. When you're stressed, a hormone called cortisol is released by the adrenal gland, disrupting the normal functioning of the hippocampus, the region of the brain responsible for working memory and learning. Forgot your keys? Can't remember the name of the book on your night table? It's not early Alzheimer's. Most likely you've been interrupted by one or more of the myriad stimuli that assault you every day. The phone rings, an SMS message chimes on your cell, or the FedEx guy is knocking at your door. Memory loss has become so common it's no longer an affliction of old age.

New York Times columnist David Brooks called this phenomenon the Great Forgetting. He said, "They say the 21st century is going to be the Asian Century, but, of course, it's going to be the Bad Memory Century. Already, you go to dinner parties and the middle-aged high achievers talk more about how bad their memories are than about real estate. Already, the information acceleration syndrome means that more data is coursing through everybody's brains, but less of it actually sticks. It's become like a badge of a frenetic, stressful life—to have forgotten what you did last Saturday night, and through all of junior high. In the era of an aging population, memory is the new sex."

Richard Saul Wurman, author of over eighty books, knows how to turn "data" into valuable information. When he wrote *Information Anxiety* in 1989, he inspired a new discipline called information architecture. He used simple examples to explain the difference between facts and information. Between memorizing and learning. For example, suppose you're interested in buying some land in order to build a house. The real estate broker tells you that the property is 115,200 square feet. You have the facts, but they have no meaning. Imagine instead that you're told that the property is equal to two football fields. Now you have information that you can understand and remember. Wurman says that "learning is remembering what you're interested in." He has proved this, anecdotally, time and again. And so have you. Ask a teenager what his mother served for dinner last night and you'll get a blank stare. Ask him who Stephen Colbert had on his show that week and he'll tell you the entire roster.

The nineteenth-century philosopher and psychologist William James would agree with Wurman. In 1890, nearly 100 years before *Information Anxiety* was published, James addressed the issue of attention in *The Principles of Psychology*. He wrote, "Millions of items of the outward order are present to my senses which never properly enter into my experience. Why? Because they have no *interest* for me. My experience is what I agree to attend to. Only those items which I *notice* shape my mind—without selective interest, experience is an utter chaos. Interest alone gives accent and emphasis, light and shade, background and foreground—intelligible perspective, in a word."

It appears that the amount of information that goes zipping around the world also conforms to Moore's law. According to MIT's *Technology Review*, the world's data traffic is doubling every two years. Who's responsible for this traffic jam? All of us. *Glut*, a fascinating book on information systems by Alex Wright, takes us on a whirlwind tour of history and tells us that "human beings now produce annually . . . more than 50,000 times the number of words stored in the Library of Congress, or more than the total number of words ever spoken by human beings." Some of the more than five exabytes come from social networking sites and user-generated content posted on sites like youtube.com and facebook.com. The self-publishing craze has done more than create a new industry for music, movies, and publishing. It's reinforced the notion that everything we write, sing, record, videotape, or draw is worthy of other people's attention. This conceit spills over into other aspects of our digital lives, especially among echo boomers. Join a site like twitter.com and you can be among the hundreds getting breaking news bulletins such as "I just washed my hair." Or "Finally finished my term paper." Of course, there are benefits. When an American graduate student at U.C. Berkeley's journalism program was about to be arrested in Egypt for taking photos at a protest rally, he "twittered" one word, "arrested," which prompted the forty-eight friends in his network to take action. James Karl Buck was released, but his Egyptian friend remained in jail for covering the event.

Simple 7 Puzzle

Will Shortz has been the crossword puzzle editor for The New York Times *since 1993. He is also the founder and director of the American Crossword Puzzle Tournament. But words are not his only passion. Numbers tickle his brain power, too, and he's the master of Sudoku puzzles. And a good thing, too. He once told me that editing crosswords had become more challenging because common knowledge was disappearing. Our society was developing information and cultural gaps that couldn't be bridged. Take music, for instance. Some of the biggest names of this century are rap artists that most puzzle doers couldn't identify. And if you did know the name of, say, Ghostface Killa, you may not know the first name of the lead singer of the Jefferson Airplane. Numbers, on the other hand, are agnostic. They are a universal language.*

Will is the one and only academically accredited "enigmatologist" in the world. He has a degree from Indiana University and studied law at the University of Virginia. But the law didn't do it for him. Puzzles did. And he was generous enough to create this one using just seven numbers for this book.

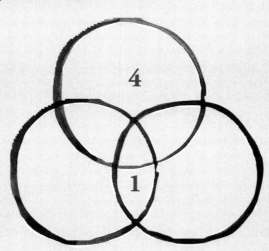

Place the digits 1 to 7 in the grid so the four digits in each circle add up to the same total. Not counting its reflection, the answer is unique.

(Answer is on page 35)

ATTENTION

A company called Big Research (which will probably have to become Gigantic Research before the end of this decade) found that the only way for people to keep up with the deluge of media options is to multitask. They claim that simultaneous media consumption of information from the Internet, newspapers, magazines, radio, TV, and direct mail is up as much as 35 percent, depending on the medium. But multitasking is stressful and inefficient. It can even be dangerous, as noted by the increase in traffic accidents resulting from people using their cell phones while driving.

In the late 1980s, when I was editor in chief of *Family Circle* magazine, one of the largest consumer magazines in the country at that time, I started a column called "Beat the Clock." The idea was to help women learn how to multitask in order to save time for themselves and their families. The editors and I thought this was a cutting-edge idea that would serve our readers well. Like other top consumer publications, the magazine invested in expensive reader research, surveying subscribers about the features and columns in every issue. When the results came back, "Beat the Clock" was at the bottom of the list. It was a dud. So we redesigned the column, changed the name, and tried again. But it still didn't work. We tried for six months before finally killing the column. What the readers knew instinctively and what we, as editors, ultimately discovered was that people don't *want* to have to do two (or more) things at once because they don't think they can do both things well.

They were right. New studies show that multitasking yields subpar results. Our minds are capable of great things, but not all at once. You might be able to play the piano and the accordion, but you can't do both simultaneously (and this is a good thing). Edward M. Hallowell, M.D., author of *Crazy Busy*, says that people can handle only two low-level tasks at once, and John Medina, Ph.D., author of *Brain Rules*, who was featured in an ABC News segment called "Life in the Slow Lane," said, "You can show that people on projects that are trying to multitask make twice as many errors and it takes them twice as long to get something done." In fact, researchers have shown that multitasking is simply a series of interruptions that keep us distracted and unable to focus. William James knew what it meant to be focused: "Everyone knows what attention is. It is the taking possession by the mind, in clear and vivid form, of one out of what seem several simultaneously possible objects or trains of thought. Focalization, concentration of consciousness are of its essence. It implies withdrawal from some things in order to deal effectively with others, and is a condition which has a real opposite in the confused, dazed, scatterbrained state which in French is called *distraction* and *Zerstreutheit* in German." James was a true scholar, but he was also a prophet of sorts. He even predicted the phenomenon of multitasking by posing the question "To how many things can we attend at once?"

Whether or not this century is called the Great Forgetting, we have certainly moved from an industrial economy to an information economy and now to an attention economy. The premise of attention economics, which is a course being offered at many top business schools, including Harvard, is that the ability of human beings to focus clearly on information and manage it is not only rare but valuable. Hence, it must be taught. At Emory University, Professor David Bray's syllabus states, "Similar to the effect of pollution on the

Earth's natural environment, information pollution can erode the limited attention spans of individuals and cause detrimental stress-related effects for both individuals and societies as a whole." He acknowledges that humans have finite attention spans, memories, and processing capabilities and concedes that more information does *not* always result in better decisions.

CHOICE

The seemingly endless choices of products, information, entertainment, even virtual friends and lovers can make you feel in control of your destiny until the glut is so overwhelming that the MEGO effect (my eyes glaze over) takes place and no action or decision is made. We become intellectually catatonic. The simple answer to this dilemma is to throw some, if not all, of the choices overboard. In *Predictably Irrational*, author Dan Ariely recalls how, in 210 B.C., a Chinese commander named Xiang Yu pulled a fast one on his troops. They awoke one morning to find their ships in flames and their food supplies ruined. They had one choice: kill or be killed. And that's how they beat the forces of their opponents, the Qin Dynasty. Wiping out distracting options in order to focus on one clear goal is a risky strategy, except, it seems, when it comes to food.

Spring, a restaurant in Paris that likes to break rules, offers a no-choice menu. Not only do the sixteen lunch and dinner guests have to eat what is served, they have to eat it at the same time. The chef, Daniel

Rose, is an American (Mon Dieu!) who serves four courses at each meal, created out of the day's fresh market offerings. He also doubles as the sommelier, pouring the wine he selects to go with his meal. The critics love the place. Even Michelin gave Spring a Bib Gourmand award for good food at moderate prices. No-choice may not appeal to everyone, but at Spring you'll wait three months for a reservation.

For some, having decisions made for them is a perfect antidote to a world of plenty. The Cosmos Diner in New York City offers, on average, 285 items 24/7. Yet patrons seem to have their favorites. In a not very scientific poll of diners, the seven most frequently ordered lunch and dinner classics are: the cheeseburger platter, the turkey dinner with all the trimmings, tuna on rye, the classic BLT, the meatloaf special, ham and cheese, and grilled cheese. "When faced with so many choices, you can't overestimate the value of the tried and true," says Kristin van Ogtrop, editor in chief of *Real Simple*. "If you love that cashmere sweater, buy it again next year. Or if you've found a line of shoes that always fits and doesn't give you blisters, why deviate? For me it's Theory pants. They always fit, and I don't have to waste time hunting for something that might not fit as well or look as good. Of course the reason that's not a good answer is it keeps you from trying new things. A satisfied life has to be about the balance of those two driving forces. Still, people should be trained to come to the 'just good enough choice' and stop! They don't need to know the rest. I would much rather go to a restaurant that has seven things on the menu than have to pore over pages of options and then listen to a waiter tell me the day's specials. That's why readers connect to *Real Simple* today. We give them the seven things."

A nother magazine, *Cooking Light,* knew their readers wanted simple recipes that could be prepared quickly with ingredients that most people would have on hand. Their feature, "Your Lucky Number: 7 Ingredients or Less" was a big hit, offering popular menus and meals. "When you make your ingredients count, there's no need to go higher than seven," they said. "These recipes will get you in and out of the kitchen with little effort. Each contains only seven ingredients (not counting salt, pepper, or water)." And naturally, they offered seven menus. My favorite recipe is the Summer Corn and White Bean Soup:

This quick, fiber-packed soup is a terrific way to use fresh corn. Add a slight kick with a sprinkle of Monterey Jack cheese with jalapeño peppers just before serving.

Yield
6 servings
(serving size: about 1½ cups)

Ingredients
- 1 tablespoon canola oil
- 1 cup sliced green onions
- ¾ cup chopped cooked ham (about 4 ounces)
- 3 cups fresh corn kernels (about 5 ears)
- ½ teaspoon salt
- 2 15-ounce cans navy beans, rinsed and drained
- 2 14-ounce cans fat-free, less-sodium chicken broth
- 2 4.5-ounce cans chopped green chilies, undrained

Preparation
Heat canola oil in a Dutch oven over medium heat. Add onions and ham, and cook 3 minutes, stirring frequently. Stir in corn and remaining ingredients. Bring to a boil; reduce heat, and simmer 5 minutes or until thoroughly heated.

When Choice is Prime

Danny Meyer is New York City's "Mr. Hospitality." He's the president of Union Square Hospitality Group, which includes Union Square Cafe, Gramercy Tavern, Eleven Madison Park, Tabla, Blue Smoke, Jazz Standard, Shake Shack, and The Modern, Cafe 2, and Terrace 5 at the newly renovated Museum of Modern Art, and, most recently, Hudson Yards Catering. His passion for food and wine is exceeded only by his love of family and his commitment to his community.

I love food. When I travel and experience a wonderful new flavor or an exceptional new dish, I'm like a little kid who just tasted his first dish of ice cream. I can't wait to eat it again. So I'll ask one of my chefs to develop a recipe and add it to the menu. I travel a lot, so I'm always trying to add things to the menus because our customers like new, inventive dishes. It's what makes our restaurants successful. But you can go too far.

Historically, my chefs would say I put undue pressure to have them try new things. You try to reach a balance in terms of what the kitchen can cook really well. If there are too many items on a menu, the food becomes a commodity, not a specialty. And the kitchen staff can't take the time truly great meals deserve. I've had to edit myself, because I've always wanted to try something new. I've learned to balance the menu in terms of the kitchen and the guests. If there's any one compliment I treasure, it's that we're consistent. Our restaurants delight your palate, but at least as much, we want the experience to be dependable. If you go overboard on too many menu items, you can undermine the entire process.

In 1994, when I opened my second restaurant, Gramercy Tavern, I knew we'd make it. Why? Because we were given the following phone number: GR 7 0777. I did not ask for that number, and in those days you didn't have to worry about a 212 area code. You hoped you'd have a number that people could recall, and I knew that they'd always remember those sevens. I remember turning to my partner and chef, Tom Colicchio, and saying, "We're in, we made it." Without having done any research on the number, I knew that seven was a lucky number. I knew it would work for us. In its second year in *Zagat*, Gramercy Tavern became the seventh most popular restaurant—a milestone. It's been the first or second for the past seven years.

On July 7, 1977, I was working at my summer job in a printing factory in St. Louis. It started at six in the morning, and I took the job because I thought it would be a good idea to have this experience. I had gotten the job because of my dad, so it was important for me not to be seen as a friend of the owner, but as a regular guy. I decided to gain favor with my fellow factory workers by joining them at the horse races in East St. Louis. We all bet the seventh horse in the seventh race that night. The horse was modestly good, not a favorite, but not two steps away from retirement. But because of the date, the horse had 2 to 5 odds. We all bonded when the horse ran dead last.

I learned good people skills early on and they've served me well in the hospitality business. I have 600 employees, and I hire people with a high hospitality quotient (HQ). I look for 49 percent technical skills and 51 percent emotional skills. Here's my list of **seven character traits that define those emotional skills:**

1 Optimism

2 Kindness

3 Curiosity about learning

4 An exceptional work ethic

5 A high degree of empathy

6 Self-awareness

7 Integrity

Emblematic Sevens

In the Bible, God's blessing on the seventh day is followed by scores of other references to seven. It was the number of Jewish feasts, festivals, purifications, and years between sabbaticals. Seven was also the number of Pillars of Wisdom, and in other cultures it was often linked with intellectual mastery. Seven was sacred to the god Osiris in Egypt (a symbol of immortality); to the god Apollo in Greece (the number of strings on his lyre); to Mithras, the Persian god of light (the number of initiatory stages in his cult); and to the Buddha (his seven emblems).
—*The Complete Dictionary of Symbols*

Eliminating options, no matter how much sense it might make at a given time, is a challenging undertaking. One reason is that we're all gamblers at heart. When we do a Google search and get 500,000 results, we don't quit after the first page or two. We think there's gold in those hills. So we dig and dig and before long we've wasted an hour or two and, as a bonus, we have a stiff neck. Besides, it's nearly impossible to eliminate possibilities. Because shutting doors—closing ourselves off from work, friends, information, tools, and entertainment—doesn't fly. Dan Ariely, a professor of behavioral economics at MIT, says that's because we're stuck in a "just in case" mind-set. He says we buy multimedia computers even though we'll never record a podcast or a video; drive SUVs even though we'll never go off-road; overschedule our kids with after-school activities even though they could learn a lot (or even more) playing freely with other children. But we do it "just in case" that piano lesson unveils a hidden prodigy. Ariely wanted to know why people were reluctant to commit to a given choice and thus eliminate other options. So he teamed up with Jiwoong Shin, a professor at Yale, and created the "door game."

The game was a computer program showing three doors: red, blue, and green. Students were given 100 clicks. Each time they entered a room, they could earn between 1 cent and 10 cents. Every time players switched rooms, they used up one of their clicks. If a room was not entered after twelve clicks, it would disappear. As the game progressed and doors diminished in size, warning players that they were about to disappear, students would revive the doors by clicking on them even though they weren't "money clicks." The players' stress levels increased, but their winnings didn't. Had they chosen to stay in one room, they would have earned more money—an interesting metaphor for life today.

Ariely calls keeping all your options open irrational excitement. Why irrational? When the students were given the equivalent of a "cheat sheet" (that is, they were told what kind of winnings to expect from each room and given time to practice) the results did not differ from the original outcomes. They did not allow the doors to close because they experienced it as an emotional loss. They became prisoners of their own choices.

Type "Internet" into Google and you'll find nearly two billion links to pore over; where are you going to even start? At, say, one minute per link, it would take more than 2,000 years to complete your search. Where is Mel Brooks's 2,000-year-old man when you need him? Or walk into a Home Depot and see how long it takes you to compare the 164 different screwdrivers they sell—and don't forget to include the near-microscopic set included in the eyeglass kit at the checkout counter.

High on Pop

7Up, which was advertised as the "uncola" in the 1970s, has a somewhat mysterious past. Its founder, Charles Leiper Grigg, had a company called the Howdy Corporation in St. Louis where Bib-Label Lithiated Lemon-Lime Soda, the original name of the product, was made. According to a professor at MIT, Grigg decided to name the drink after the atomic mass of lithium, 7, which was one of the ingredients in the original formula. Lithium citrate, the mood-stabilizing drug, might have made the soda a hit, since it launched two weeks before the stock market crash of 1929.

Consider the following:

- There are over 100 million blogs that even the bloggers' mothers don't have time to read.

- Tropicana orange juice choices went from two (container and frozen) to more than seventeen: orange pineapple, orange tangerine, orange strawberry banana, Pure Valencia, Pure Valencia with Pulp, Pure Valencia with Mango, low acid, Healthy Heart, Healthy Kids, Antioxidant Advantage, Pulp Free Calcium plus Vitamin D, High Pulp plus Calcium, Light 'n Healthy with Calcium, Light 'n Healthy with Pulp, High Pulp, Some Pulp, No Pulp.

- And if you wanted to treat every piece of clothing you own with the respect it deserves, you'd have to buy twenty-six different detergents from Tide alone.

There's an old joke about a new immigrant who was learning to speak English. He would stop at a coffee shop each day and order the same thing: apple pie and coffee. One day his friend said in their native tongue, "Why don't you try a little variety? Order a ham sandwich and coffee." The newcomer was grateful for the advice. So the next day he went to the coffee shop and told the waitress, "Ham sandwich and coffee." She said, "Do you want that on white or rye?" He replied, "Apple pie and coffee."

How many times have you felt like the immigrant when you've walked into a Starbucks and found yet another exotic choice from Sumatra or Madagascar served as caramel macchiato?

Unless you're an expert, it's the same confusion you experience at a fine restaurant when the waiter hands you the wine list at the beginning of the meal, or brings the tea box at the end. Yes, tea is the new coffee, and at Hina's in Sacramento, California, you have your choice of over 250. The owners acknowledge that the sheer number of teas is at first overwhelming to their customers, so they provide information and tastings to help them distinguish among the choices.

No wonder John Maeda titles the introduction of his book "Simplicity = Sanity." The American Psychological Association would agree with him. In a series of experiments published in the *Journal of Personality and Social Psychology*, researchers, headed by Kathleen D. Vohs of the University of Minnesota, found that making many choices impairs self-control. They determined that making a choice uses the same brain resources that are used for self-control and active responding. The more subjects were forced to make choices among products, courses of study, and other options, the less they were able to meet deadlines, possess physical stamina, or soldier on against adversity. In short, too many choices paralyzed the subjects.

W hy has Google become the dominant search engine on the Internet when it was launched four years after Yahoo!? Take a look at the opening pages of Google and Yahoo! and decide which is simpler, easier to focus upon, and easier to use.

To this day, experts claim that Apple would have dominated Microsoft in the world market if Steve Jobs had opened his operating system to software developers early on. Talk to anyone who owns a Mac and

they'll tell you that it's a more elegant machine with a friendlier interface than a PC. Buy an iMac, plug it in, push one button on the back of the screen, and you're ready to use your new toy. Buy a desktop and it's an hour—at least—crawling around on the floor as you fiddle with the power adaptors of the multiple components. People have responded to Apple's simple design by increasing Apple's computer market share.

For average consumers, a successful technology product is simple and intuitive, something even a child could use. Of course children have set the rules when it comes to judging the value of a new gadget, game, or tool. Their mantra is: "If I have to read the manual, it wasn't built right." They, like us, want to keep things simple.

Here are seven simple ways to a smarter, simpler life:

❶ **YES:** Ask for help, pay for help, or say yes to an offer of help.

❷ **NO:** Learn how to say no to too many social engagements, too many favors, too many extra projects at work; too many irrelevant solicitations from spammers and direct mailers.

❸ **STOP:** The clock. Life isn't a 24/7 merry-go-round. If it were, you wouldn't get the seven hours of sleep necessary to keep you fit and sane.

❹ **GO:** Keep in shape with an exercise routine you can stick to.

❺ **START:** Use technology so it doesn't use you up. Online banking, for instance, will save you time, money, and stress because your mortgage will be paid automatically.

❻ **END:** Clear the clutter, trash the trivial stuff. Get organized.

❼ **BE:** Make time for friends, lovers, family. Learn how to breathe and daydream. Be your true self and find your humanity.

PRIME TIME

One of the simplest ways we manage money is using credit, debit, and ATM cards. But the theory behind this technology was discovered more than 2,300 years ago when one man with a knack for numbers figured out that not all numbers are created equal. The great Euclid was the first to prove that prime numbers are the building blocks of all other numbers, which led to the natural question: How many prime numbers are there? It was Euclid who first proved that there is an infinite number of primes. His discovery allows you to use your ATM card or debit card without getting ripped off.

Who cares? Even though we might not see prime numbers every day, the fact remains that we use them all the time. The most popular encryption methods that are employed to protect the sensitive information we send over the Internet involve the subtle idiosyncrasies of prime numbers.

These seemingly unbreakable codes comprise an area now known as public key cryptography. Finding the prime divisors of whole numbers in general is very tricky business. The key idea behind these subtle mathematical encryption schemes is that factoring a very large number into primes is very difficult. Of course factoring is easy if the number is small, say 35: we see that it is the product of 5 and 7. But what if the number was a bit larger, say 30,796,045,883? Even if we were told that this number is the product of exactly two different prime numbers, it is not obvious what those primes are. Thus, this large number holds a

secret. In these clever encryption schemes, the large numbe
encode information, but it is those secret prime numbers that are used
to decode the encrypted data. Even computers cannot find the primes
associated with numbers containing hundreds of digits—thus those
codes appear to be "unbreakable." (By the way, in our example, it turns
out that 30,796,045,883 is the product of the primes 163,841 and
187,963—multiply them and see for yourself.)

The knowledge that there is no end to the primes implies that, at
least for the time being, we can always create unbreakable secret
codes. So often in human history, what appears abstract and devoid
of purpose today will be the central key to simplifying our everyday
lives tomorrow. —*Edward B. Burger*

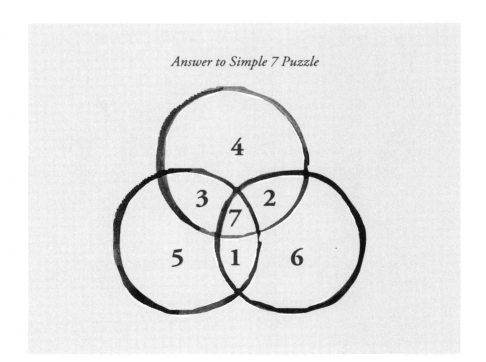

Answer to Simple 7 Puzzle

BUNNY HOP

*Eastern cottontails share habitats with seven other
cottontails and six species of hares. Females can have seven
litters a year, producing as many as thirty-five young.*
—Source: Smithsonian National Museum of Natural History

CHAPTER 2

Happiness

Happiness makes up in height for what it lacks in length.
—Robert Frost (1874–1963)

Ask yourself or your friends what makes them happy and you'll get the usual answers: the love of family and friends, peace of mind, good health, financial security, and so on. Some get more philosophical, saying happiness is the absence of sadness. But when a friend told me it's the ability to savor and extend joyful moments, I thought he was on to something. I probed a bit more and he said, "Happiness is losing yourself in the moment so that time stands still." To clarify: He was not talking about ecstasy—sexual rapture or great triumph—but he could have been describing the way you feel leading up to those moments. He was talking about flow, the revived buzzword for being in the zone. The relatively new field of positive psychology, popularized by Martin Seligman of the University of Pennsylvania, claims there are three roads to happiness, which is described as deep contentment: pleasure (having fun, feeling joy), flow (losing yourself in the moment), and meaning (what Rick Warren calls the Purpose-Driven Life). Perhaps true happiness comes from all three of these ideas working together. You can lose yourself in preparing a spreadsheet sales analysis for a tobacco company, but it isn't fun or good for humanity and is unlikely to make you happy.

"The best moments in our lives are not the passive, receptive, relaxing times.... The best moments usually occur if a person's body or mind is stretched to its limits in a voluntary effort to accomplish something difficult and worthwhile," says Mihaly Csikszentmihalyi, a director at the Drucker School at Claremont University. He and others have described the **seven "feelings of flow":**

1. We have total involvement and focus, complete concentration on a chosen task.

2. There are clear goals.

3. We have deep, effortless involvement.

4. There is a sense of control.

5. Intrinsic motivation—whatever produces "flow" becomes its own reward.

6. Our sense of self vanishes.

7. Time stops.

Being in "flow" means having sustained focus, with no distractions, no interruptions. Nothing can break your concentration. If your average day is filled with ringing phones, e-mail alerts, and other interruptions, you'll never get to flow. Here's where the number seven becomes a filter for happiness. Limiting the number of tasks on your daily "to-do list" to seven can free you to get to flow. Overscheduling your day, your kids, and your life is the fundamental enemy of flow. Dr. Tal D. Ben-Shahar teaches positive psychology at Harvard, one of the most popular courses offered. He says, "Simplify! We are, generally, too busy, trying to squeeze in more and more activities into less and less time. Quantity influences quality, and we compromise on our happiness by trying to do too much." Yet Americans love to be busy because being busy makes people feel valued and useful. But being too busy can undermine happiness.

Millions of people watched Tiger Woods play the last round of the 2008 U.S. Open as he walked the ninety-one holes, wincing with almost every step, at Torrey Pines Golf Course in California. He had a tear in his ACL (the ligament that controls and stabilizes the knee and tibia), and stress fractures in his tibia. This was one injury that couldn't be ameliorated by taking three Advil before playing. He played five rounds, limping and clutching his knee all the while before finally winning his fourteenth career championship in a sudden-death playoff. Every time he took a swing, every time he pivoted on his left leg, the pain had to be excruciating. How did he do it?

In an earlier interview with *60 Minutes*, Woods credits his ability to handle stress and pain with his powers of concentration. "I mean, your concentration is so high, so keen. Because all this pressure's on you. Your senses are more heightened. Everything seems to flow better. It's a great feeling," he explains. Athletes call it being "in the zone." But with Tiger, that zone has its own zip code. *New York Times* columnist David Brooks described the difference between Tiger and his popular opponent, Rocco Mediate: "Rocco Mediate's head swiveled about as he walked up the fairway of the sudden-death hole of the U.S. Open on Monday. Somebody would catch his attention, and his eyes would dart over and he'd wave or make a crack. Tiger Woods's gaze, on the other hand, remained fixed on the ground, a few feet ahead of his steps. He was, as always, locked in, focused and self-contained."

When I lived in Singapore, one of my newspaper colleagues invited me to attend a Hindu ritual called Thaipusam. This is celebrated by Tamil Indians in Malaysia and Singapore who want to thank the god Murugan for the good fortune that may accrue to them. In order to show their devotion, some of them pierce their skin with hooks and drive skewers into their tongues and cheeks as they climb the many steps to the temple. But unlike Christian flagellants, they don't bleed and they appear to feel no pain. In fact, like Tiger Woods, they are

A Thaipusam devotee

focused on their task, believing that the mind can control the body. Having witnessed this amazing test of faith and endurance, I came to believe they're right. You may think that Thaipusam is a form of self-inflicted torture. But as I chanted for my friend's cousin and watched his body being pierced repeatedly, I saw in the man's eyes a look of intense concentration and purpose. He was convinced that his sacrifice would be rewarded. Just like Tiger Woods.

Eastern philosophy has guided Tiger Woods throughout his life. He's a Buddhist who says that his religion has given him self-awareness. He's also learned patience, a virtue of leadership and maturity. Some sports psychologists think that it's Tiger's focus, his ability to concentrate and avoid distractions, that makes him a champion. I believe it's also what makes him happy. So I asked Josh Waitzkin, the famed chess player, if he thought Woods was happier while he was playing the game, or afterward, when he won. Without missing a beat, Josh said unequivocally that Woods was happier playing the game.

Josh Waitzkin is a winner in every way that word implies. When he was nine years old he won his first national chess championship and never stopped perfecting his game, dazzling the chess world by claiming title after title. After his father wrote a book about him, which eventually became the movie *Searching for Bobby Fischer*, Josh became a teenage media star and had to learn how to keep his focus in a world complicated by celebrity. *Searching for Bobby Fischer* is a snapshot of Josh's life as a boy, as a son of loving parents, as a champion. But it doesn't explain this brilliant young man's search for happiness, and the journey that helped him find it.

When he was twenty-one, Waitzkin took on a new challenge: Tai Chi Chuan. Once again, Waitzkin mastered this elegant combat and spiritual quest and won many championships. By competing in the martial arts—ostensibly an entirely different discipline than chess—he

---

Just Whistle a "Happy Number"

A happy number is a number that ends in one after squaring its digits. Huh? Start with the number 7, for example, and square it (49). Then take the 4 and the 9, square those numbers, and add them up. Do it again and again. If you get to number one, you've not only multiplied and added correctly, you've discovered a happy number!

Start with 7: $7^2 = 49$; $4^2 + 9^2 = 16 + 81 = 97$; $9^2 + 7^2 = 81 + 49 = 130$; $1^2 + 3^2 + 0^2 = 1 + 9 + 0 = 10$; $1^2 + 0^2 = 1$!

was able to deconstruct the elements of winning and losing and create a modern philosophy, a fusion of Eastern and Western thought. He calls it "the art of learning" and, now in his early thirties, Waitzkin has told his story in a book by the same name.

One of the principles in Waitzkin's book is focus. As a child chess prodigy, he had to learn how to cope with random sensory distractions like the sound of an ambulance going down the street or the physical tics of an opponent. For most of us, continued distractions and interruptions can become frustrating. "You are concentrated on the task at hand, whether it be a piece of music, a legal brief, a financial document, driving a car, anything. Then something happens. Maybe your spouse comes home, your baby wakes up and starts screaming, your boss calls you with an unreasonable demand, a truck has a blowout in front of you." Waitzkin explains that if you're in the hard zone, straining to fight these distractions, you are in trouble. "Like a dry twig, you are brittle, ready to snap under pressure." The alternative, he explains, is what sports psychologists call the soft zone. It's where Tiger Woods lives because no random event—no change of wind or weather, no shout from a fan, no sound of a clicking camera—can undermine his focus or ability to recover after a bad shot. He is flexible where others are brittle.

Arbor Day

In Mesopotamia, the earth and heaven were divided into seven zones and the Tree of Life had seven branches.

Seven Weeks That Changed My Life

In addition to Josh Waitzkin's intense competitive life, he teaches learning and performance psychology. Josh published his first book, **Attacking Chess,** *at age eighteen, and his latest book,* **The Art of Learning,** *was published in 2007. He recently founded the JW Foundation, which is dedicated to helping parents and teachers nurture the unique potential of young children.*

When my hand shattered I felt the shock burn through my body, down into the ground, and then a wave of calm followed. Time slowed down. On the video I see an angry 230-pound bruiser trying to tear me apart, shooting his hands at me like bullets. It looks scary, to be honest, but in the moment it was beautiful. His attacks stopped to a crawl, rolled towards me like clouds. I was sixty pounds lighter and fighting for my life with one hand, but the next forty-five seconds were the most peaceful I had ever known.

The following day the doctor shook his head over X-rays and told me I could forget about defending my national title seven weeks later. Even if my bone healed, the muscles would have atrophied too much to take tournament-level impact. I nodded and was back on the mats that night. Something had clarified in me. I had felt the power of mind. How could I make time slow down without breaking a bone or flinging myself down a flight of stairs? As the weeks passed, I trained with one arm and meditated, visualizing the workout moving from my healthy side to the arm that was immobilized in a cast. I resolved not to atrophy and I didn't. But more importantly, I made a plan.

I competed in that Nationals a couple days after getting my cast off, and I managed to win. Then I put my plan into gear. In the past seven years, that wild moment in the ring has been a beacon in my martial arts training and in my approach to learning in general. It has won me world championships and it has taught me to find exquisite pleasure in the subtlest ripples of my life. It is about simplicity, really—plunging deeply into small pools of information, then linking the pools, dissolving complexities into a sense of intuitive flow where my conscious mind can look at less and see it in more detail, in bigger font, or in more frames than before. Anyone can do it, and it can be applied to any pursuit. All it takes is a little bit of patience and a whole lot of love.

THE PHILOSOPHERS

I n his book *The Happiness Hypothesis: Finding Modern Truth in Ancient Wisdom,* Jonathan Haidt takes ten great ideas from different civilizations and explores how those ideas have been adapted to a modern world. Living a life of virtue, meaning, happiness, and love is described by the masters of moral thought: Aristotle, Socrates, Buddha, and Confucius, to name a few. Greek philosophers defined happiness in ways that still resonate today. They represented different schools of thought and ultimately different disciplines and areas of study. Their wisdom is derived from the Seven Sages, ancient thinkers known as the founders of Greek philosophy. The sages were Thales of Miletus, Pittacus of Mitylene, Bias of Priene, Cleobulus the Lindian, Myson the Chenian, the Spartan Chilon, and Solon of Athens. Solon was known as the lawmaker, and although he was born into a well-to-do family, he had contempt for the rich. This poem is credited to him.

> The man whose riches satisfy his greed
> Is not more rich for all those heaps and hoards
> Than some poor man who has enough to feed
> And clothe his corpse with such as God affords.
> I have no use for men who steal and cheat;
> The fruit of evil poisons those who eat.
> Some wicked men are rich, some good men poor,
> But I would rather trust in what's secure;
> Our virtue sticks with us and makes us strong,
> But money changes owners all day long.

Among the late Hellenic philosophers, here are seven giants. The first three share the common metaphysical belief that **virtue and wisdom lead to happiness:**

❶ SOCRATES believed that true happiness requires self-knowledge; that self-knowledge presupposes virtuous actions; that virtuous actions lead to happiness.

❷ PLATO said truth and reason were the key to happiness. He believed that ideas and a rich intellectual life could lead to self-fulfillment.

❸ ARISTOTLE espoused eudaemonism, a kind of ultimate happiness resulting from living a rational life focused on the pursuit of excellence.

❹ PYTHAGORAS was the numbers man. He invented his own mathematical theorem and held that numbers could illuminate the music and rhythm of the universe. He believed in the transmigration of the soul, so his numerical quest was likely for the pattern or scale that would lift his soul upon death, leading to absolute happiness.

❺ EPICTETUS was a stiff-upper-lip kind of guy. He harks from the school of Stoicism and believed that one's life is determined by fate rather than will. He advocated grace under pressure and a dispassionate reaction to negative circumstances. As a result, one would find happiness.

❻ EPICURUS is misrepresented in the United States. We assign him to good food, good times, and a kind of Bacchanalian lifestyle. Nothing could be farther from the truth. Epicurus believed that happiness resulted from the absence of pain and that pleasure should be tempered because overindulgence would bring unhappiness. Like other ethicists, he thought that virtue was the key to happiness and that friendship could bring stability and tranquility.

❼ ZENO OF CITIUM believed in the natural order of life and that happiness was derived from accepting that order. He believed that this reasoning would bring inner peace.

The one who would be in constant happiness must frequently change.
—Confucius

Ancient philosophers like Confucius had a different view of happiness than the modern West. In Asia, the individual is less important than the group or community. Being happy, therefore, is impossible if those around you are suffering.

Over 2,500 years ago Confucius knew that adaptability was the key to leading a happy and successful life. If your fields are always wet, plant rice instead of wheat; if gas is over four dollars a gallon, carpool; if the Santa Anas are blowing at Pebble Beach, spread your feet wider to stabilize your putt.

Here are Confucius's **seven ways to the good life**, adapted from an article in the *Journal of Happiness Studies* by Dr. Zhang Guoqing, Zhejiang University, China, and Prof. Dr. Ruut Veenhoven, Erasmus University, Rotterdam. They concluded that ancient Confucianism can help a modern person find happiness.

> **❶ Love and be loved** Confucianism's view of life is built on the idea of "Jen." This means a feeling of concern and compassion for others. Generally speaking, marriage makes us happier, more friends make us happier, and people are especially happy if they can share their life—warts and all—with someone.

❷ Participate in your community, your world Confucianism encourages its followers to engage in society. This is also good advice because people who are members of clubs, churches, and other organizations are happier; people who work are happier, and so on.

❸ Work hard Confucianism recommends a commitment to your occupation. The wealth earned from working is also seen in a positive light within Confucianism. Generally speaking, people with more money and higher status are happier (but more money doesn't always equal more happiness).

❹ Have fun, experience pleasure Confucius thought moderate amounts of fun were acceptable. (I guess that translates as more than a chuckle but less than a guffaw.) And, big surprise, research shows that people who engage in pleasurable activities are happier!

❺ Respect your body Still in the realm of the blindingly obvious, people who are healthier are happier. Obvious or not, people throughout the developed world are becoming overweight; we think pills will cure everything; people are still abusing drugs and alcohol; and few of us get enough exercise.

❻ Seek knowledge and wisdom This could also translate as "indulge your curiosity." Educated people are more likely to get better jobs, which could contribute to happiness, but having lots of degrees doesn't necessarily bring you satisfaction and joy.

❼ Be responsible One of the most important aspects of ancient Chinese Confucianism is a sense of duty and responsibility. There's sparse evidence that this might lead to greater happiness. At a societal level, however, people who live in collectivist societies, like the Chinese, tend to be less happy than those who live in individualistic societies. This may be because collectivist societies stifle the individual's search for self-actualization.

A 2008 World Values Survey showed that people and countries could actually increase happiness. From 1981 to 2007, levels of happiness rose in 45 of the 52 countries the survey measured. When Americans think they can change something, they go at it with a vengeance. That's why happiness has become an industry.

You can read more than 296,598 books on the subject of happiness, and if you really want numbers, search "happiness help" and you'll come up with some 50,000,000 choices. The obvious areas of health, wealth, love, friendship, and faith are standard fare in most self-help books and magazines. But there's one relatively new area that isn't on the standard list, and it can boost your happiness by 25 percent. That's gratitude for you. Literally. Dr. Robert A. Emmons, professor of psychology at University of California, Davis, conducted a series of research studies for his book *Thanks! How the New Science of Gratitude Can Make You Happier.* Whether young or old, the results were the same: practicing gratitude made people happier. Clearly, this is not about everyday manners. It's about acknowledging that teacher who took the time and trouble to help you pass algebra. Or writing a letter to your

You Can't Shake It Off...

A study in the *International Journal of Psychophysiology* measured the effects of anger over a seven-day period. On the seventh day, the blood pressure still rises when people recalled their frustration or confrontation. All the more reason to chill out.

parents or other relatives and expressing your heartfelt thanks for all they have done for you.

Few people ever bother to express a real thank-you, save for the standard "bread and butter" letter after a gift is given. That could be because thanking people is acknowledging that you needed them on your road to success or happiness. That you couldn't get there on your own. And our egos don't usually allow us to be that generous. Practicing gratitude forces us to take an honest look at our lives and the people who support us. Being "thankful" is a little like finding forgiveness.

The number seven is the perfect tool for balancing your life and finding happiness. Think of seven as a skateboard.

If you added one more thing to either end, you would tip the balance. You'd have to add items by twos, fours, or more to be in perfect balance, but then you'd be overwhelmed with a to-do list that was unachievable. The key to a happy life is learning how to say no to the myriad choices that confront you. Will you attend the club's meeting? Can you help your friend move her office? Your husband wants to start a blog and needs you to be his tech support. All of these things can be done, but only on your terms and within your seven-a-day, seven-a-week priority list.

CAN MONEY BUY HAPPINESS?

Give a child a toy he's been asking for and you'll see something akin to pure joy on his face. He'll play with it almost obsessively until he knows it too well. Soon the toy goes to the bottom of the chest, never to be played with again. But are adults much different? The thrill of a new car, a beautiful dress, or the latest iPhone can wear off quickly, leaving you hungry for "more." Psychologists wanted to know if happiness is having what you want, wanting what you have, or both. Jeff Larsen from Texas Tech University and Amie McKibban of Wichita State University surveyed their undergraduates and found that people who want what they already have are happier than those who did not value their possessions. You'll be happier if you stop thinking about trading up to that three-bedroom condo across the street. As Warren Buffett put it: "Success is getting what you want, happiness is wanting what you get."

Richard Easterlin, an economist at the University of Pennsylvania, argued in a 1974 paper that economic growth does not necessarily lead

---

A guy joins a monastery and takes a vow of silence: he's allowed to say two words every seven years. After the first seven years, the elders bring him in and ask for his two words. "Cold floors," he says. They nod and send him away. Seven more years pass. They bring him back in and ask for his two words. He clears his throat and says, "Bad food." They nod and send him away. Seven more years pass. They bring him in for his two words. "I quit," he says. "That's not surprising," the elders say. "You've done nothing but complain since you got here."

to more satisfied citizens. With the exception of going from abject poverty to having basic necessities, people living in countries with steady economic growth from 1950 to 1970 showed no increase in happiness. He did acknowledge that relative income—and the status that implied—had a more profound effect on people than financial security. When it comes to money, houses, and automobiles (except when gas is at an all-time high) most of us are children after all, as in, "Mine is bigger than yours!"

B ut recently two economists, also from the University of Pennsylvania, have challenged Easterlin's thesis. Betsey Stevenson and Justin Wolfers found that absolute income matters more than relative income. They cite a Gallup Poll that shows that people in households making $250,000 or more a year call themselves very happy compared with households with income of less than $30,000. A 2005 *Time* magazine poll showed similar results.

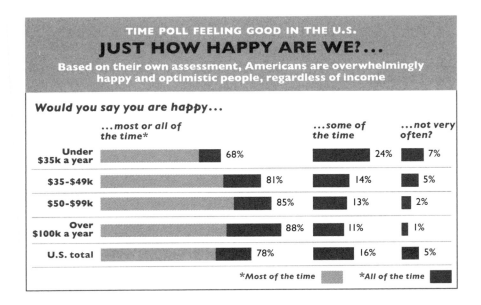

TIME POLL FEELING GOOD IN THE U.S.
JUST HOW HAPPY ARE WE?...
Based on their own assessment, Americans are overwhelmingly happy and optimistic people, regardless of income

Would you say you are happy...

	...most or all of the time*	...some of the time	...not very often?
Under $35k a year	68%	24%	7%
$35-$49k	81%	14%	5%
$50-$99k	85%	13%	2%
Over $100k a year	88%	11%	1%
U.S. total	78%	16%	5%

*Most of the time   *All of the time

Of course what this entire debate is missing is the idea of money as a marker of success rather than as a source of acquisition. According to one of the participants, Warren Buffett told students from Emory and UT Austin, "I'm the ultimate freeloader. I don't need multiple houses. If I wanted to do something wild and crazy I could do it, but Anna Nicole Smith is gone. Reminds me of the story of the sixty-year-old man that got a twenty-five-year-old to marry him. When his friends asked how he did it, he replied, 'I told her I was ninety.'"

Buffett continued: "I know a woman in her eighties, a Polish Jew woman forced into a concentration camp with her family, but not all of them came out. She says, 'I am slow to make friends because when I look at people, I have one question in mind: Would they hide me?' If you get to be my age, or younger for that matter, and have a lot of people that would hide you, then you can feel pretty good about how you've lived your life. I know people on the Forbes 400 list whose children would not hide them. 'He's in the attic, he's in the attic.' Some of them keep compensating by joining board seats or getting honorary degrees, but it doesn't change the fact that no one will give a damn when they are gone. The most powerful force in the world is unconditional love. To hoard it is a terrible mistake in life. The more you try to give it away, the more you get it back. At an individual level, it's important to make sure that for the people that count to you, you count to them."

Heads Up

There are seven holes in the human head.

Buffett is as rich in wisdom as he is in liquid assets. But make no mistake: he planned on being rich all along. And, according to Israel Vicars of Fast Company, he has **seven principles on living a life of simplicity and happiness:**

❶ Happiness comes from within.
"In my adult business life I have never had to make a choice of trading between professional and personal. I tap-dance to work, and when I get there it's tremendous fun."

❷ Find happiness in simple pleasures.
"I have simple pleasures. I play bridge online for twelve hours a week. Bill [Gates] and I play, he's 'chalengr' and I'm 'tbone.'"

❸ Live a simple life.
"I just naturally want to do things that make sense. In my personal life too, I don't care what other rich people are doing. I don't want a 405-foot boat just because someone else has a 400-foot boat."

❹ Think simply.
"I want to be able to explain my mistakes. This means I do only the things I completely understand."

❺ Invest simply.
"The best way to own common stocks is through an index fund."

❻ Have a mentor in life.
"I was lucky to have the right heroes. Tell me who your heroes are and I'll tell you how you'll turn out to be. The qualities of the one you admire are the traits that you, with a little practice, can make your own, and that, if practiced, will become habit-forming."

❼ Making money is the by-product of our guiding purpose.
"If you're doing something you love, you're more likely to put your all into it, and that generally equates to making money."

I f you have a great idea, along with the passion, energy, and drive to see it through, maybe you should be the employer instead of the employee. In the late 1980s my partner Mary Anne Sommers and I started our own business—a beautiful, glossy magazine called *Child*. At that time, the only competing publication was *Parents*, then a smart, basic "how to diaper your baby" bible printed on cheap paper and geared to a mass audience. *Parents* was (and is) the gold standard in the category. But we wanted to appeal to an educated reader who had already read Dr. Spock, someone who wanted to learn about Bruno Bettelheim's theories of fantasy and how traditional fairy tales affect a child's mind. We illustrated stories like that with gorgeous photos from famous photographers like Patrick Demarchelier and Jean Pagliuso. A few things fell into place right away, including our partnership. Mary Anne's background was in ad sales, mine was in editing and journalism. Together we filled the two essential jobs of magazine publishing: publisher and editor in chief. But we were savvy enough to know that a solid partnership depends on a solid legal agreement.

The first order of business was developing a strategic plan and "dummy" pages to show to potential investors. But neither of us had the experience to create the financial analysis. My contacts—my friends—were invaluable to this process. One of them, Mortimer Zuckerman, a magazine and newspaper publisher, met with us many mornings to guide us in developing "the numbers." When we had all the pieces of our business plan together—the concept, the marketing plan, the potential advertiser list, and the financials—we took the plan to some of the biggest publishing houses in the magazine business, companies like Time, Inc., Condé Nast, Hearst, and Meredith, looking for investment money and a home for *Child*.

There was mild interest, but no one stepped up to the plate until Mary Anne was contacted by Italian publishers who wanted her to help launch a beautiful fashion magazine that they were introducing in the U.S. called *Taxi*. When she told them she couldn't work with them because she was committed to our new venture, they said "We'll publish both." We were ecstatic. We hired a wonderful small staff of talented pros who didn't expect big salaries and didn't need remedial training in magazine publishing. As beautiful and surprising as the magazine was, few knew about it because it was printed at a plant in Milan, crated onto a boat, and shipped to New York Harbor. Sometimes the cargo would be quarantined for days, even weeks, making us miss our newsstand dates, forcing the distributors to return the bundled magazines unopened. We also learned that the printer had not been paid. Here's where our lawyer proved his worth beyond orchestrating our partnership agreement.

Our deal with the Italians included a clause that said if they reneged on payments to suppliers or contributors, the full ownership of the magazine would revert to us. They reneged. We got custody of our *Child* and, in a stroke of luck, we sold the magazine to the New York Times Company a few months before the stock market crash of October 1987. We wouldn't have gotten to square one without these **seven strategies to a successful start-up:**

❶ **THE IDEA:** In an age when ideas are commodities, yours has to be unique and serve an identifiable audience.

❷ **PARTNERS ARE A PLUS:** If you can be a one-man band, fine. But if you're not Superman or Wonder Woman, you'll probably benefit from a partner or partners, even if they don't have equal ownership. It's good to bounce ideas off people you trust. And they don't always have to be family, like the Johnson brothers (Johnson & Johnson). Some famous partners: Sergey Brin and Larry Page (Google); Ben Cohen and Jerry Greenfield (Ben & Jerry's); Bill Hewlett and Dave Packard (Hewlett-Packard); Richard Warren Sears and Alvah C. Roebuck (Sears, Roebuck).

❸ PASSION AND DRIVE: Investors look for a number of things: Is your idea unique? Is your business plan complete and well thought out? Are you trustworthy and professional? And, perhaps most important, do you have the passion and drive necessary to sustain a start-up?

❹ THE RIGHT LAWYER: Don't underestimate the value of a good lawyer, someone who's well versed in contract law and has experience in your field.

❺ CONTACTS COUNT: Share your idea with trusted friends and business associates, and get as much advice as you can about their own businesses, failures, and successes. They can introduce you to potential investors, staff, and other business resources.

❻ THE BUSINESS PLAN: At the very least, creating a business plan is a reality check. If you've never created an Excel spreadsheet, start practicing, because you'll want to see different iterations of costs and revenue over a five-year period before you start touting your business proposition.

❼ THE STAFF: The people you hire will make or break your business. They should have clear job responsibilities and share your passion and vision.

The number seven comes up in multiple business strategies. *Forbes* can tell you the seven best ways to get a raise. *Fortune Small Business* elaborates on the seven great ways to finance a start-up. Bankrate shows you how to be a millionaire in seven easy (ha!) steps, and CNN Money has seven ways to fight property taxes. There are hundreds of "seven strategies" for making, saving, and spending money, but none of this will bring you true happiness. Having enough money to live a civilized life and educate yourself and your children is a good thing, but it's not number one on the list of happiness. The results of economist Glenn Firebaugh's research showed that while money makes the cut, physical health was the best single predictor of happiness, followed by income, education, and marital status.

HEALTH AND HAPPINESS

The health-happiness connection works both ways. As Confucius said, healthy people are happier and, according to new research by Ruut Veenhoven of Rotterdam's Erasmus University, happy people may live from 7.5 to 10 years longer than the average sourpuss. Veenhoven compared thirty studies carried out over the last sixty years and concluded that the effects of happiness on longevity were similar to the effects of not smoking. That doesn't mean that if you quit smoking *and* you're happy you're automatically guaranteed a life that will be longer by fifteen or twenty years, but, just in case, the American Lung Association offers a terrific book, *7 Steps to a Smoke-Free Life*. They also want you to know why you smoke, and they've identified **seven common reasons why people are still puffing away:**

1. You're under a lot of stress at work.
2. All of your friends are smokers, so you can't escape it.
3. Smoking helps you keep your weight down.
4. You really have a strong addiction to cigarettes. You have trouble going an hour without one.

❺ You really enjoy smoking. It is pleasurable for you.

❻ You don't have the willpower to quit.

❼ Smoking helps you feel relaxed and positive.

Years ago, when I learned I was pregnant with my daughter, I immediately decided to quit smoking, which was a real challenge, since I had been a heavy smoker. I got a booklet from the American Lung Association and began following the steps. My husband and I went to dinner with Avery and Judy Corman one evening, and I bragged that I was down to half a pack a day. Judy was one of my best friends, and she asked me why I had started smoking. I told her that some of the coolest girls in my junior high school taught me how to smoke at a seventh-grade dance. Like most kids, I wanted to fit in. Judy owned a children's store in those days, and when I came home from work the next day, there was a package from Judy. In it were a sweet little quilted baby heart, a package of gum, and a handful of sugar-free hard candy. There was also a letter, which read:

> Dear Jackie:
>
> I cannot believe that you're still smoking even though you're pregnant. Don't you know that you're harming your baby? Don't you know that you look ridiculous with a cigarette in your mouth and your belly out to here? You are, dear friend, a social disgrace, and I urge you to quit before you do permanent damage.
>
> > Your loving friend,
> > Judy

At first I was furious. This was the most insulting letter I had ever received from anyone, let alone a close friend. But Judy knew that since I started smoking for social reasons, I'd quit for exactly the same reasons. She was right. I never smoked again. The American Lung Association should follow her lead and tell smokers the truth: that smokers are doomed to become pariahs. And if you really want to prevent killer diseases and a heart attack, quitting smoking is a no-brainer. Lowering cholesterol is also important, but it's no longer the ultimate demon. Chronic inflammation now has that dubious distinction, and a substance called C-reactive protein (CRP) is the measuring stick. Here are *Men's Health* magazine's **seven "do's,"** **adapted for both sexes:**

❶ Drink your OJ or take your vitamin C; the vitamin that can reduce CRP.

❷ Eat fish like mackerel, tuna, salmon, and bluefish because the omega-3 fatty acids in them can also reduce CRP.

❸ Consume at least twenty grams of fiber, which can lower cholesterol and keep your body in tune. Think ABC every day: an *apple*, a slice or two of whole grain *bread*, and a cup of high-fiber *cereal*.

❹ Do the obvious: Lose the weight through diet and exercise and you'll reduce more than your waistline.

❺ Keep it up so you don't get down, because depression may exacerbate inflammation. Stay in close contact with friends and family, and don't let the green monsters of life get you.

❻ Floss at least once a day because tooth infections can travel up, down, and sideways, and could cause the kind of inflammation that can't be easily controlled.

❼ Follow the Romans and Greeks and use olive oil instead of butter.

Michael Roizen, M.D., chief wellness officer at the Cleveland Clinic, says olive oil may turn off the gene that makes the pro-inflammatory molecules that attach to your arteries. In addition to his contributions to *Men's Health*, Dr. Roizen is a co-founder of realage .com, and has partnered with Dr. Mehmet Oz to write a number of bestselling books about consumer health, including *YOU: The Owner's Manual*. Michael follows medical science to the letter of the law, but he has a soft spot for the number seven. He has a painting of the number in his office because he thinks it brings him luck, and he confided that he's a sucker for the movie classic *The Magnificent Seven*. "I saw it forty-nine times during my years at Williams—as did almost every other student at Williams during my era—twelve times a year during exams plus one extra senior year."

❦

Hey, Baby!

The average weight of a newborn baby is 7.5 pounds.

Hearts and Minds

Seven has a place in partner Mehmet Oz's life, too.

Dr. Mehmet C. Oz is professor and vice chairman of surgery at Columbia University and director of the Cardiovascular Institute and the Complementary Medicine Program at New York Presbyterian Hospital.

I decided to be a heart surgeon at age seven. My dad and I were on line at Patterson's ice cream store in Wilmington, Delaware, about fifteen minutes from our house. Dad loves ice cream. Ahead of us was a nine-year-old boy and Dad asked him, "What are you going to be when you grow up?" The boy said, "I have no idea." That was a problem for Dad because the boy hadn't thought about it.

Dad was a thoracic surgeon. And this was the year that Christiaan Barnard, a friend of Dad's, had performed the first human-to-human heart transplant. He loved the idea that a heart transplant could be done. It meant a lot to him that we could go where no man had gone before. He went into the field not just to manage people who were ill, but because he knew he would be part of one of the most amazing breakthrough eras in modern medicine. The spiritual symbolism of the heart was also important to Dad.

What made my dad most special was that he grew up in central Turkey in abject poverty during the Depression. He had nothing. Getting an education was nearly impossible. But his parents imprinted on him the importance of knowledge. They insisted that he go to school and study hard. He did so well that he was sent here, to the U.S., to further his education.

Not having a direction in life was intolerable to him. So my life changed at age seven when the nine-year-old came up short and then Dad asked me the same question. I used to make rounds with my father—it was legal back then. His patients appreciated what Dad had done for them. I knew what it would feel like to be a doctor. So I said, "I want to be a heart surgeon."

Just to emphasize: My dad didn't necessarily want me to be a heart surgeon. He wanted me to pick a direction. Wandering aimlessly would not allow me to practice at anything. My whole life has been aiming at things. I wanted to play pro sports. So I aimed at that. I wanted to be part of the media. So I worked at that, too. You organize yourself, find mentors, and you don't give up. My father proclaimed that even if I changed my mind, I should always be aiming at a goal. I guess I made the right choice because I never changed my mind.

THE HAPPIEST MAN I EVER KNEW

What was remarkable about Ed Ateyeh was what he wasn't. He wasn't rich; he wasn't handsome; he wasn't tall; he wasn't healthy in the classic sense; he wasn't famous. Ed lived a life that millions today are searching for. A life of purpose and meaning, filled with the seven important aspects of life: love, family, joy, work, friendship, faith, and humor. He had polio as a child and walked with a limp. I remember his strange shoes because one was built up on the inside to adjust for his crippled leg. He was a contractor in the Garment Center in New York City. When the designer robe manufacturers couldn't handle the orders, they outsourced the work to Ed. His workers were like his family: black and Puerto Rican men and women who were as hardworking and loyal to Ed as he was to them. I know this because I worked there for two summers when I was a kid, trimming threads and turning belts outside in on the fleece robes that we manufactured under the Halston label. If one of his workers was sick, Ed would send a basket of food and make sure that the family was taken care of. He attended all the weddings, confirmations, and communions that his workers invited him to. But he wasn't just a "boss." He was a worker, too. He sat at a machine just like "the girls" during busy times and sewed the pre-cut fabric into women's robes. He was the fastest piece worker in his own factory.

Ed's kids, Michele and Edward, and his wife, Elaine, loved hosting summer barbecues for friends and lavish Christmas dinners for family. As full as his life was, Ed never seemed rushed or hassled. He stopped working at 7 P.M. every day. He knew his limits, and because he managed his life, controlling the interruptions, dismissing the unnecessary, he was happy and joyful. I remember **seven little things that always made him happy:**

1 A new bloom on his prize tulips

2 Playing with his dog

3 The children on his lap

4 A newfound Edison wax cylinder for his collection

5 An afternoon game of pinochle with his friends

6 Catching a big fish

7 Driving his neighbor to get twice-weekly dialysis

He's All Ears

A study in the *British Medical Journal* claimed that men's ears grow in seven-year cycles into old age. The authors, Jos Verhulst of the Louis Bolk Institute in the Netherlands and Patrick Onghena of the University of Leuven in Belgium, found that ears reach their peak growth velocity every seven years, followed by a hiatus. The likely reason for the growth? Gravity. Note: The researchers didn't factor in the possibility of cross-dressing and wearing heavy clip-on earrings.

Seven Around-the-World Balancing Acts

❶ CHINA

❷ CANADA

❸ PHILIPPINES

4 SOUTH AFRICA

5 BRITAIN

6 AFGHANISTAN

7 INDONESIA

KISS AND TELL

Hawaii's Seven Sacred Pools, aka O'heo Gulch, tickle the body with gentle waterfalls that spew fresh water into the pools that flow into the ocean. In the movie I.Q., Meg Ryan said the pools were like 1,000,000 kisses on your skin.

CHAPTER 3

Love

Gravitation cannot be held responsible for people falling in love. How on earth can you explain in terms of chemistry and physics so important a biological phenomenon as first love? Put your hand on a stove for a minute and it seems like an hour. Sit with that special girl for an hour and it seems like a minute. That's relativity. —Albert Einstein, 1879–1955

When hundreds of people filed into a Manhattan auditorium to hear a memorial service honoring Clay Felker, an iconic magazine editor, they expected to be regaled with untold stories of Clay's coverage of the power elite, his fostering of "the new journalism," and his high-flying social life. Tom Wolfe, Gloria Steinem, Lesley Stahl, Milton Glaser, Richard Reeves, David Frost, and others did not disappoint. We were supposed to take away an indelible picture of a man who had reinvented the modern magazine. Instead, most of us left the service realizing that we had just heard a great love story.

Clay was married to Gail Sheehy, whose best-selling books and magazine articles made her one of the most sought-after authors and speakers in the literary world. After a seventeen-year on-again, off-again courtship, the gravitational pull of love became undeniable to both Gail and Clay, and they agreed, in 1984, to marry. As Gail explained in an article in

Tango magazine, they had entered their "settling down stage." They adopted a Cambodian child and Clay renovated his imposing co-op apartment. It was an A-list New York life—busy, on the go, sought after. Seven years later, Clay was diagnosed with throat cancer. The virulent kind. Clay's doctor advised them to plan on fighting the disease by living a new dream, employing new strategies, and focusing solely on their love and his recovery. Two years later, they moved to the University of California at Berkeley, where Clay started a magazine center at the Graduate School of Journalism.

That passage lasted another seven years, when Clay's health deteriorated further, and once again they moved, this time from their heavenly house in the hills to a simple condo where their life could be managed. Eventually they came back to New York, where Gail continued as Clay's primary caregiver. At this point Clay had a feeding tube, but that

Love in a Time of Ephemera

Gail Sheehy is AARP's Ambassador of Caregiving. Her latest book, The Caring Passage, *will be published soon.*

Clay sat tall and straight in his wheelchair and for the next hour and a half drank in the music as his sustenance. His attention locked on Mike Melvoin, the jazz pianist whose trio it was, an older man, with undiminished passion. He had been playing piano since he was three years old and was still, past seventy, composing didn't stop Gail from planning a trip to Paris as if they were honeymooners. She convinced the chef of a top restaurant to blend food so Clay could ingest it. The chef not only agreed, he provided a screen for privacy and arranged for the food to be served in silver pitchers.

In the last year of his life, Clay had a permanent trach tube in his throat and could speak intelligibly only to, or through, Gail. Ultimately, Gail decided to provide professional palliative care at their home. "It was really, really rough. The key was putting control back into Clay's hands," Gail said.

When it was clear that Clay was nearing his "final deadline," as Gail put it, she asked him if he wanted to go out and hear some jazz, his favorite music. In an e-mail to their friends, Gail described this magical evening, one of the last of Clay's life.

for movies and TV. He was another of those indefatigable creatives, like Clay, who produced his first publication at the age of eight, the *Greeley Street News*, and sold it up and down his block in Webster Groves, Missouri, for the up-market price of a nickel. Melvoin voiced the philosophy behind his original compositions.

"There's a lot of pessimism and feelings of futility out there.... It's the job of music to dispel those feelings. This is a little song called 'Life is What You Make It.'" Up-tempo drums kick-started a piece with strong major chords and a restless back beat. Melvoin leaned in to the keyboard and swayed passionately up and down the octaves with his hands crossing and fingers flying, turning music into the thunder of life. Clay's fingers drummed on the table...he was a drummer as a boy.

Between two aides, myself, and a cooperative driver, we cantilevered Clay out of the car and back up to the apartment and into bed shortly before midnight. He was not the least tired. He wanted to talk. He gripped my hands and said clearly, with gusto, "It was a wonderful evening."

Clay died a week later.

G ail and Clay sustained their love because Gail filtered the vast number of choices in her life in order to focus on Clay and their marriage. She had seven key priorities: Clay's physical and mental health; their home; her work; his work; their children and grandchildren; their friends; and, ultimately, herself.

That list may be common, but Gail didn't let anything interfere with her focus. They didn't adapt to the world as if they had lost a great battle; they found a way to make the world adapt to them.

The Seven Percent Solution

A study by sociologist Michael Rosenfeld at Stanford University showed that 7 percent of the 59 million married couples in the U.S. are interracial. In 1970, that number was 2 percent. Tiger Woods, George Lucas, Ellen Pompeo, Wolfgang Puck, and Eva Longoria have all tied the interracial knot.

Then Harvard professor George Miller published his seminal paper in 1956, "The Magical Number Seven, Plus or Minus Two: Some Limits on Our Capacity for Processing Information," he was living in a world that was far less complex, far less interruptive than the one we know today.

Home media capacity 1956

Broadcast TV, land line phone, hi-fi, am/fm radio, snail mail, newspapers, magazines

Home media capacity 2008

Broadcast, cable, satellite, IP TV; DVR; land line, cell phones; CDs, DVDs; broadcast, digital, satellite radio; hi-fis, stereos, mp3s; PCs/Macs; newspapers, magazines, snail mail, e-mail; game consoles, portable games, online games; pagers, PDAs; digital cameras; Internet, social networks, cloud computing, virtual worlds; broadband, wireless access, mobile computing; smart appliances, GPS systems

Seven media items in 1956; thirty-five in 2008.

Known as the father of cognitive science, Miller showed, and others confirmed, that short-term-memory capacity in the human brain is limited to about seven digits, letters, words, or other elements. "Everybody knows that there is a finite span of immediate memory and that for a lot of different kinds of test materials this span is about seven items in length," Miller wrote. His work is far more complex than this simple statement, of course, and is especially relevant in today's always-on world. Since the brain dictates how much information it can hold in short-term memory, what happens when it receives too much information? The goal of receiving information is, after all, to produce communication or "output." That is, we have learned something from the stimuli we have received and we can analyze and transmit it in significant ways. Miller called this the measure of input-output correlation. But if that input is overwhelming, and we begin to guess at or estimate the output because of confusion, we are risking far more than accuracy. We are risking our well-being.

In today's world, the number seven is more than a definition of short-term-memory capacity. It's a filter for a saner, happier life. By limiting distractions and the barrage of stimuli, we're able to perceive the rich and subtle signals that define us, like nonverbal communication from our partners, our children, our colleagues, and our friends. When it comes to love, using seven as a filter allows us to *listen* rather than simply *acknowledge*. And we can use the filter to boost sensory perception:

If This Is Your Life...	...Try This
Touch screen, keyboard	Touch one another
Look at images on a screen	Look into her eyes
Listen to songs on your iPod	Listen to him
Talk on a cell phone	Talk face to face

In her book *Distracted*, Maggie Jackson describes a fascinating study by Elinor Ochs, a MacArthur Fellow and head of UCLA's Center on Everyday Lives of Families. A linguistic anthropologist, Ochs studied thirty-two demographically diverse families for seven years. According to Jackson, Ochs found that "wives stopped what they were doing and welcomed home a returning spouse only a little more than a third of the time. Mostly they were too irritable or busy to do so. Husbands did better, with more than half offering a positive greeting to a spouse." No one expects a wife to welcome hubby home in a flimsy see-through nightie, martini in hand, but blatant rudeness and disregard resulting from distraction is a twenty-first-century behavior that does not bode well for the future of the species.

G ail and Clay could have been the poster couple for The Gottman Institute in Seattle, Washington, where love, marriage, and divorce are studied by founders Drs. John and Julie Schwartz Gottman. Gottman was a contributor to *Reader's Digest* when I was editor of that magazine. Every month he would deconstruct and analyze a marital problem based on his best-selling book *The Seven Principles for Making Marriage Work*, as well as case histories from his "Love Lab." Over the years, he focused on the success factors of long-term marriages like Clay and Gail's. In addition to his "principles," Gottman identified **seven signs of happy couples** in *New Scientist* magazine:

❶ Getting and giving love and affection

❷ Nurturing and supporting one another through the vicissitudes of life

❸ Having and showing respect for one another

❹ Liking one another to the point where being together makes time flow like wine (See Chapter Two, "Happiness," p. 37.)

❺ Finding it easy to be together (This sounds basic, but some couples are actually uncomfortable with one another. They don't share the same brand of humor, the same references, the same customs and manners, and those differences can pull them apart.)

❻ Liking yourself when you're together

❼ Creating a sense of shared purpose, meaning, and values

Gottman has made love into a science. Trained as a mathematician, he creates formulas based on the universal gestures, expressions, and movements of couples in his Love Lab and uses them to predict whether the marriage will succeed or fail. He claims a 91 percent accuracy rate. "Happily married couples aren't smarter, richer, or more psychologically astute than others. But in their day-to-day lives, they have hit upon a dynamic that keeps their negative thoughts and feelings about each other (which all couples have) from overwhelming their positive ones. They have what I call an emotionally intelligent marriage," Gottman says.

Emotionally intelligent people know how to interpret their partner's unspoken language and consciously decide to act on the information—or not. A change in voice tone, dropping one's eyes, hunched shoulders, sighing more than usual—these may be signs of a down day or worse. If you're the partner, you have two choices: ignore the symptoms or act on them. Sometimes the action can be a simple indirect gesture. My father liked a special seven-layer cake that my mom made occasionally. There never seemed to be a particular reason for her to bake that cake, so one day I asked her and she said she baked it to put a smile on Dad's face. This recipe, from Neiman Marcus, comes close to matching Mom's special treat:

Seven-Layer Cake

- ¾ cup shortening
- 3 ⅓ cups cake flour
- 2 ¼ cups sugar
- 4 ½ tsp. baking powder
- 1 ½ tsp. salt
- 1 ½ cups milk
- 3 eggs
- 2 tsp. vanilla

1. Stir shortening just to soften.
2. Sift in dry ingredients.
3. Add 1 cup of milk; mix until all flour is dampened.
4. Then beat vigorously for 2 minutes.
5. Add remaining milk, eggs, and vanilla.
6. Beat vigorously 2 minutes longer.
7. Pour 2 cups batter into a lightly greased and floured 9x1½-inch round pan. Tip pan so batter runs over bottom.
8. Invert pan over baking sheet and tap edges on baking sheet, allowing as much batter to run out of pan as will do so easily.
9. Turn pan right side up, scrape down sides to prevent burning, and even out batter remaining on bottom.
10. Repeat for other 6 layers, baking as many at a time as you have pans and oven space.
11. Bake at 400° for 8 minutes or till done.
12. Cool in pans for 3–5 minutes, then invert on rack to cool. Put layers together and frost with Chocolate Butter Frosting.
13. While baking first layers, keep remaining cake batter in refrigerator.

Chocolate Butter Frosting
- 3 cups confectioners' sugar, sifted
- ⅓ cup hot water
- 4 oz. (4 squares) unsweetened chocolate, melted
- I egg, lightly beaten
- ½ cup butter or margarine, softened
- I ½ tsp. vanilla

1. Blend sugar and hot water into melted chocolate.
2. With spoon beat half of egg into chocolate mixture; beat in remaining egg; beat in butter, a tablespoon at a time.
3. Blend in vanilla.
4. Frosting will be thin at this point, so place bowl in pan of ice water and beat until spreading consistency.

The American Speech-Language-Hearing Association (ASHA) has identified seven behaviors in nonverbal communication that emotionally intelligent people should know about.

There are seven classes, also known as codes, of nonverbal signals. Codes are distinct, organized means of expression that consist of both symbols and rules for their use. Although these codes are presented within classes, they occur together and are naturally integrated with verbal expression. The nonverbal codes include:

❶ **KINESICS**—messages sent by the body, including gestures, facial expression, body movement, posture, gaze, and gait

❷ **VOCALICS** (i.e., paralinguistic)—vocal cues other than words, including volume, rate, pitch, pausing, and silence

❸ **PHYSICAL APPEARANCE**—manipulable cues related to the body, including hairstyle, clothing, cosmetics, and fragrance

4 **HAPTICS**—contact cues, such as frequency, intensity, and type of touch

5 **PROXEMICS**—spatial cues, including interpersonal distance, territoriality, and other spacing relationships

6 **CHRONEMICS**—the use of time as a message system, including punctuality, amount of time spent with another, and waiting time

7 **ARTIFACTS**—manipulable objects in the environment that may reflect messages from the designer or user, such as furniture, art, pets, or other possessions

Interpreting these behaviors is something we all do, usually without acknowledging it. Imagine you're at a meeting and a woman starts twirling her hair (kinesics). Chances are the boss is infantilizing her and others by undermining the authority of the staff. A well-known former news magazine editor was one of the few women who had risen to a high position on the masthead in the 1980s. She was short in stature and spoke in what could be described as a whisper (vocalic). This forced her colleagues—especially the men—to bend over in order to get close enough to hear what she was saying. Was this a conscious tactic, a passive-aggressive behavior, or simply a physical quirk? You don't have to explain haptics to most women when it comes to male sexual advances. But the subtle gestures that men show to other men often reveal a kind of dominance. When a man puts his arm on the shoulder of another man, he's suggesting that he has paternal power over the son. You often see U.S. presidents show their dominance over other heads of state with this gesture.

We all have friends who are never on time (chronemics). Chronic lateness has been linked to adult ADHD, but it may be a planned event, according to psychologist Willard Gaylin. He describes a patient in his book *Talk Is Not Enough* who was always ten minutes late for her appointment. She would begin the session with "Sorry I'm late." One day Gaylin told her she wasn't late because she had planned on arriving ten minutes after the hour. He had identified her secret control mechanism. After that, he said, her lateness became erratic until eventually she took responsibility for being punctual.

Proxemics was introduced by anthropologist Edward Hall in the 1960s as a way of describing how people interact through their spatial relationships. He had a set formula for the space we occupy, and separated that space into four areas: intimate space, personal space, social space, and public space:

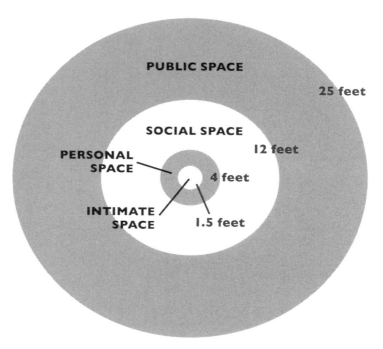

Most of us have a problem when our intimate space is violated by people who don't have our permission to be there. We see this behavior as aggressive and intrusive, and we tend to reject the interloper.

In *Blink: The Power of Thinking Without Thinking*, Malcolm Gladwell claims that all of us have the ability to read people and situations in mere seconds based on first impressions. We "blink" when we meet people for the first time; when we hear music; when we walk into someone's home. And when it comes to elections, we blink and blink again, judging candidates on all seven behavior signs. In the 2008 election, for example, Sarah Palin elicited an instant and dramatic response—negative and positive—based on at least four of the seven nonverbal codes: hand gestures (kinesics); hairstyle and eyeglasses (physical appearance); speech (vocalics); and the "baby," whom many thought she carried like a prop at photo ops (artifact).

Knowing how to interpret nonverbal signals and act on them appropriately with a loved one is neither an intuitive gift nor a talent. It's an act of will that can keep love relationships healthy and thriving. How do I love thee? If you take the time to count the ways in Elizabeth Barrett Browning's poem, there are—you guessed it—seven:

How do I love thee? Let me count the ways.

❶ I love thee to the depth and breadth and height
My soul can reach, when feeling out of sight
For the ends of Being and ideal Grace.

❷ I love thee to the level of everyday's
Most quiet need, by sun and candle-light.

❸ I love thee freely, as men strive for Right;

4 I love thee purely, as they turn from Praise.

5 I love thee with a passion put to use
In my old griefs, and with my childhood's faith.

6 I love thee with a love I seemed to lose
With my lost saints,—

7 I love thee with the breath,
Smiles, tears, of all my life!—and, if God choose,
I shall but love thee better after death. [Can't count this;
it's in the future!]

If you were limited to only romantic, passionate, or erotic love, life might be exciting, but it wouldn't be rich and fulfilling. The ancient Greek philosophers knew that our capacity to love one another, to love living creatures, to love and appreciate the mysteries of life, to love beauty, enhanced our humanity. **Love between lovers is one of seven kinds of love:**

1 Between Lovers

2 Between a Parent and Child

3 Between Siblings

4 Between Friends

5 Between a Person and His Pet

6 Love of Self

7 Love of God

Sociobiologists, anthropologists, sociologists, psychologists, and theologians like to deconstruct the pure passion and emotion behind the various kinds of love, i.e., we're driven to find a mate in order to breed and maintain the species; or loving a pet is a substitute for loving a child; or friendship results from the primitive need to form groups for survival. Philosophers, on the other hand, look at the nature of love by embracing a variety of disciplines, including epistemology, politics, and ethics. Eros (erotic love) defines passion and desire. Plato, however, theorized that eros stood for the love of beauty, an ideal in itself.

Philia, by comparison, represents the love of friends (including our furry friends), as well as love of self. In his *Rhetoric*, Aristotle defines philia as acting in another's best interests without expecting anything in return. Since both parties must share this ethos in order to have friendship, there must be reciprocity.

The purest form of love is unconditional love or agape, a perfect description of a parent's love of a child, and other familial relationships. This pure form of love was later applied to the love of God in both the Old and New Testaments. Although they were not monotheistic, the Greeks allude to the perfection of love as a divine quality.

LOVING A CHILD

In the late 1980s, when baby boomers were begetting what has become the massive generation of "millennials," I asked Linda Arking, whose fiction has been published in the *New Yorker*, to write an essay on motherhood for *Child*. Here's a brief excerpt that describes the love mothers have for their children.

On Motherhood

This is a love story.

There's a woman on the beach, beyond an age to flirt with lifeguards. She sits alone on a towel (we see a thermos and a pile of brightly colored plastic odds and ends) gazing out to sea. And because she seems sophisticated, we fantasize about her life.

We look a little closer.

Slightly flabby thighs, hair graying at the roots. Her old high school boyfriend, now the pretzel king of western Pennsylvania, would probably shake his head, pained at the deviations from her teenage silhouette. "What happened?" he'd ask, regarding the still-youthful, barely lined face. And this looking out to sea—is this cloud watching? Daydreaming? Remembering that college summer she traveled deck class through the Aegean? Or the time she quit a perfectly good job and hopped a freighter to Morocco?

Ah, no, it's much more down-to-earth: A child, two children, are swimming out there and she doesn't dare lift her eyes from them.

Now we understand.

Knowing, then, that she's someone's mother, what else do we know? That she doesn't trust lifeguards. Nor bus drivers, nor babysitters, nor anyone entrusted even fleetingly with the lives of her children. Her paranoia along these lines began one day when, strolling contentedly up Madison Avenue, her pregnant belly wrapped in an oversize coat, she suddenly thought: *How do I know that taxi on Eighty-sixth Street isn't going to jump the curb and hit me?*

Here's what else we know: Her life was changed forever by pregnancy and birth. *She's* been changed forever (the pretzel king is right), and chronology now falls into Before and After. Sleeping late, leisure time, Morocco are all Before; a hovering protectiveness comes After.

She'd give her life for her child.

BROTHERS AND SISTERS
WE ARE SEVEN

A simple Child,
That lightly draws its breath,
And feels its life in every limb,
What should it know of death?

I met a little cottage Girl:
She was eight years old, she said;
Her hair was thick with many a curl
That clustered round her head.

She had a rustic, woodland air,
And she was wildly clad:
Her eyes were fair, and very fair;
Her beauty made me glad.

"Sisters and brothers, little Maid,
How many may you be?"
"How many? Seven in all," she said
And wondering looked at me.

"And where are they? I pray you tell."
She answered, "Seven are we;
And two of us at Conway dwell,
And two are gone to sea.

"Two of us in the church-yard lie,
My sister and my brother;
And, in the church-yard cottage, I
Dwell near them with my mother."

"You say that two at Conway dwell,
And two are gone to sea,
Yet ye are seven!—I pray you tell,
Sweet Maid, how this may be."

Then did the little maid reply,
"Seven boys and girls are we;
Two of us in the church-yard lie,
Beneath the church-yard tree."

"You run above, my little Maid,
Your limbs they are alive;
If two are in the church-yard laid,
Then ye are only five."

"Their graves are green, they
may be seen,"
The little Maid replied,
"Twelve steps or more from my
mother's door,
And they are side by side.

"My stockings there I often knit,
My kerchief there I hem;
And there upon the ground I sit,
And sing a song to them.

"And often after sunset, Sir,
When it is light and fair,
I take my little porringer,
And eat my supper there. ➤

Wily Miley

Miley Cyrus, aka Hannah Montana, had a hit
song called "7 Things." The lyrics are
pretty lame, but, as with many other musical
artists, seven is the number of choice.

"The first that died was sister Jane;
In bed she moaning lay,
Till God released her of her pain;
And then she went away.

"So in the church-yard she was laid;
And, when the grass was dry,
Together round her grave we played,
My brother John and I.

"And when the ground was
white with snow,
And I could run and slide,
My brother John was forced to go,
And he lies by her side."

"How many are you, then," said I,
"If they two are in heaven?"
Quick was the little Maid's reply,
"O Master! we are seven."

"But they are dead;
those two are dead!
Their spirits are in heaven!"
'Twas throwing words away; for still
The little Maid would have her will,
And said, "Nay, we are seven!"

—William Wordsworth, 1798

The little cottage girl may have had an unqualified love for her siblings, but that is rarely the case. Jealousy and rivalry often trump love and devotion. When we are children, these feelings are magnified by the perceived attitude of our parents. A July 2006 *Time* magazine cover story reported a series of new studies describing the impact siblings have on shaping our lives. "From the time they are born, our brothers and sisters are our collaborators and co-conspirators, our role models and cautionary tales. They are our scolds, protectors, goads, tormentors, playmates, counselors, sources of envy, objects of pride," wrote Jeffrey Kluger in *Time*'s "The New Science of Siblings."

Love between siblings is a long and complicated process that seems to grow and mellow with age. Perhaps we seek out our adult siblings, fearing "orphanhood" as we anticipate the inevitable demise of our parents. Or maybe we want to reconcile childhood rivalries and misunderstandings. That's what happened to Marie Brenner, whose latest book, *Apples and Oranges*, delves into her complicated relationship with her brother—her biological and psychic opposite. "We have a history of stupid arguments, minuscule fissures, and black holes. Our relationship is like a tangled fishing line. We are defined by each other and against each other, a red state and a blue state, yin and yang," she wrote. Her brother was dying of cancer, and he wanted to erase his life by destroying all of his memorabilia—every letter, memo, book, print, possession. But Marie wouldn't let that happen. She went to live with him, searching for two things: a cure to his cancer, and a cure to their relationship. She achieved the latter.

"Brothers and sisters are often frozen in amber, playing out roles stamped on them in their most formative years," Marie told me. "Why this happens is mysterious but it can feel like an endless bad movie— kids fighting in the backseat of the car. Our families are a laboratory of so much of what happens to us in later life. This is only one of a long list of What I Had Wished I Knew Then. Carl and I were lucky—we

Love 'em and Leave 'em: Seven Ways

Paul Simon had the world thinking that there were "50 Ways to Leave Your Lover."

But if you count them, there are seven:

1. Slip out the Back, Jack
2. Make a New Plan, Stan
3. No Need to Be Coy, Roy
4. Just Listen to Me
5. Hop on the Bus, Gus,
6. Don't Need to Discuss Much
7. Drop off the Key, Lee
   (Get yourself free)

learned we had the deepest and most profound need for one another. We wasted so much time. For decades, we defined ourselves as opposites and only later learned how much we had in common."

Kluger says, "One of the greatest gifts of the sibling tie is that while warmth grows over time, the conflicts often fade. After the shooting stops, even the fiercest sibling wars leave little lasting damage. Indeed, siblings who battled a lot as kids may become closer as adults—and more emotionally skilled too, often clearly recalling what their long-ago fights were about and the lessons they took from them."

There are **seven positive love signals that parents give or withhold** and, ironically, these same seven signals can forge the lifelong bonds between brothers and sisters:

1. **UNQUALIFIED LOVE** (spoken and gestured)

2. **RECOGNITION**

3. **ACCEPTANCE**

4. **APPROVAL**

5. **COMPASSION**

6. **ATTENTION**

7. **RESPECT**

Like many American families, mine is blended. My stepdaughters, Karen and Kristin, are eleven and thirteen years older than Alexandra. We would all be together on alternate weekends, but that wasn't enough for Alex. At about age two, she invented two imaginary friends whom I suspected were compensating for her missing siblings. After the older girls graduated from college and began their adult lives, Alex must have intuited a critical window of opportunity—either schmooze them or lose them. She chose the former, calling them, e-mailing them, constantly keeping in touch, and building a relationship that might have been marginalized had it not been for her singular efforts. Her need to love and be loved by her sisters was fundamental.

Jeffrey Kluger summed it up: "In a world that's too big, too scary and too often too lonely, we come to realize that there's nothing like having a band of brothers—and sisters—to venture out with you."

Seinfeld on Seven

When I told a friend I was writing this book, he said "You have to include the *Seinfeld* episode on the number seven." As some of you may recall, George is engaged to Susan and he had promised the widow Mantle that he would name his daughter Seven in honor of Mickey Mantle's number. Jerry says, "Seven? Yeah, I guess I could see it. Seven. Seven periods of school, seven beatings a day. Roughly seven stitches a beating, and eventually seven years to life. Yeah, you're doing that child quite a service."

Seven Siblings

Kristin van Ogtrop is editor in chief of Real Simple, *one of the most popular and successful magazines published by Time Inc. She lives in New York with her husband, who is also a magazine editor, their three sons, a shedding dog, a very old cat, a few hamsters (they come and go), and a handful of fish, which, unfortunately, never last long.*

My dad was one of seven, and getting together with his siblings was always fun—even a bit magical. I grew up in Delaware and had a very typical childhood compared to what theirs had been, because they grew up on the island of Aruba. Even after they moved to the States, the stories of life in Aruba were incredible: someone was always doing something kind of excessive—staying out too late or playing practical jokes or hitting three home runs in a baseball game. There was such "abundance" in the family, and a wonderful sense of camaraderie, fun, and family. This sense of abundance informed the choices I made in my life. I tried to model who I wanted to be on this group of people who had the greatest sense of fun—living life to the fullest.

There have been a few moments in my adult life that crystallized how I tried to pattern myself off of those seven siblings; moments that captured the joy and exuberance that I felt in their presence. Here's just one: in Aruba, my dad and his family grew up listening to steel drum music. When I got married my fiancé and I decided to have a steel drum band at our wedding. One of those crystallizing moments was on the dance floor, dancing to the steel band and watching all seven of them go under the limbo bar.

My husband and I now have three children. (I'm also one of three.) I had my first at thirty-one, the second at thirty-four—and our last nine years later. Why that final child? In part because I would look around my table when there were just four of us and I knew someone was missing. I knew we wouldn't have seven, but having three kids was driven by this group of people who were my role models. My family isn't nearly as big, but now it feels complete.

LOVING A FRIEND

I'm not going to suggest that you limit your total number of friends to a mere seven. But if you return to Edward Hall's proxemics graphic, you'll see how small your circle of intimacy truly is. Having lots of friends is easy ever since the word *friend* became a verb. Arianna Huffington, author and founder of the political website the Huffington Post, has 5,000 friends, according to her page on Facebook. But her "bffs" can be counted on her fingers. Social networking sites like Facebook, MySpace, and Twitter are seductive, especially when you receive an e-mail saying that So-and-So "added you as a friend." These sites offer lots of other benefits, like finding long-lost college roommates, playing virtual games with friends and family members, and promoting your latest project to your nearest and dearest. The 2008 presidential campaign became known as the "Facebook Election" when candidates began marketing themselves to their anonymous friends. That's no surprise to David Kirkpatrick, author of *The Facebook Effect.* "Facebook is a hugely important innovation in technology because it allows us to more efficiently communicate with people from throughout our lives; but the notion that we can really have many hundreds of 'friends' is a fallacy. Typically, as a baby boomer, most of my own small number of truly good friends remain off of Facebook, to my regret. Nonetheless I have about 700 'friends' there."

How would Aristotle, the philosopher who said "A friend to all is a friend to none," define a sea of virtual friends? They wouldn't fit into his definition of having friends that give us pleasure, although playing a great game of Scrabble with a pal online may do that for some. They might fit into the category of utility, since you can alert your entire friend database about your karaoke party. But they wouldn't make the cut for Aristotle's ideal of true friendship: shared goodwill. This selfless form of friendship can only be achieved when goodwill is reciprocated.

True friendship is like exuberant primary colors. Sadly, those colors are fading as we become too busy or too distracted to make a phone call or drop a handwritten note to a friend who landed a new job or perhaps lost one. Instead, we dash off a quick e-mail, as impersonal and obtuse as a form letter. Marginalizing friendship has serious consequences—you wind up diminishing yourself. **Using seven as a tool to restore those friendships can enhance your life in seven significant ways.**

❶ Friends make you healthier: a buddy will diet with you, meet you at the gym, swim, run, or play sports.

❷ Friends are your connectors: to jobs, apartments, other people, blind dates.

❸ Friends boost your self-esteem by encouraging you, coming down on your side.

❹ Friends get you through the rough spots: divorce, death, job loss.

❺ Friends make you smarter by sharing what they learned about the latest movie, software, art exhibit.

❻ Friends offer a respite from responsibility by being playful.

❼ Friends help you live longer.

ritish anthropologist Robin Dunbar claims that our brains are built to accommodate about 150 friends. (His actual calculation was 148.) He theorizes that there is a direct correlation between brain size and the size of social groups, which accounts for humans having more friends than tree frogs. By Dunbar's measure, if we were sizing up dolphins, we would probably refer to their social groups as graduate schools of marine mammals because they are the number-two big-brained species. The "encephalization quotient" (EQ) is a complicated formula measuring brain size and body weight. The brains at Bryn Mawr published this data:

SPECIES	EQ
Man	7.44
Dolphin	5.31
Chimpanzee	2.49
Rhesus Monkey	2.09
Elephant	1.87
Whale	1.76
Dog	1.17
Cat	1.00
Horse	0.86
Sheep	0.81
Mouse	0.50
Rat	0.40
Rabbit	0.40

Source: http://serendip.brynmawr.edu/bb/kinser/Int3.html

Still, maintaining "goodwill" friendships with 150 people in today's overscheduled, overwhelming world is nearly impossible, especially for women, who have high expectations when it comes to reciprocity.

Friends, Romans...

Plutarch of Chaeronea had a profound influence on moral and ethical behavior. His essays "Checking Anger," "The Art of Listening," "How to Know Whether One Progresses to Virtue," were part of Moralia, *a collection that became a road map to civil behavior.* Parallel Lives, *his portraits of Greek and Roman heroes, also focused on character and morality.*

A strong mutual friendship with many persons is impossible. Just as rivers whose waters are divided among branches and channels flow weak and thin, so affection, naturally strong in a soul, if portioned out among many persons becomes utterly enfeebled. We do not maintain that our friend should be "the only one," but along with others let there be some "child of our elders" and "late-begotten," as it were, not as is the fashion nowadays, by which many get the name of friend by drinking a single glass together, or by spending a night under the same roof, and so pick up a friendship from inn, gymnasium, or market-place.

True friendship seeks after three things above all else: virtue as a good thing, intimacy as a pleasant thing, and usefulness as a necessary thing, for a man ought to use judgment before accepting a friend, and to enjoy being with him and to use him when in need of him, and all these things stand in the way of one's having many friends; but most in the way is the first (which is the most important)—the approval through judgment.

We ought therefore not to accept readily chance acquaintances, or attach ourselves to them, nor ought we to make friends of those who seek after us, but rather we should seek after those who are worthy of friendship.

Now it is a fact that the enjoyment of friendship lies in its intimacy, and the pleasantest part of it is found in association and daily companionship. What is commonly called having a multitude of friends apparently produces the opposite result. For friendship draws persons together and unites them and keeps them united in a close fellowship by means of continual association and mutual acts of kindness.

On the other hand, having a multitude of friends causes disunion, separation, and divergence, since, by calling one hither and thither, and transferring one's attention now to this person, now to that, it does not permit any blending or close attachment of goodwill to take place in the intimacy which moulds itself about friendship and takes enduring form.

In his book *Friendship: An Exposé*, Joseph Epstein suggests limiting the number of people in your "inner circle" to preserve intimacy and trust. Can you really be a virtuous, good friend to more than seven people?

Y ou complete me," a line from the movie *Jerry Maguire*, is one that both Aristotle and Henry David Thoreau would have liked. Thoreau subscribed to the ideal that love and friendship should result in one person enhancing another's life. His poem "Friendship" offers this verse:

> And each may other help, and service do,
> Drawing Love's bands more tight,
> Service he ne'er shall rue
> While one and one make two,
> And two are one.

Bok Joy

Derek Bok is the former president of Harvard University. His wife, Sissela, is an author.

When Sissela and I were planning to be married in 1955, we became enamored of the idea of having the ceremony on May 5, since our wedding date would then be forever remembered as falling on 5/5/55. Thereafter, it so happened that one of our heroes, Pierre Mendès-France, agreed to marry us, as he was empowered to do by virtue of his position as mayor of Louviers (not far out of Paris). Alas, however, Mendès-France could not marry us on May 5, since he was busy with the affairs of the French National Assembly, but he could do it on May 7, a Saturday. We quickly decided that having Mendès-France officiate was much more important than 5/5/55. And so it was that we were married on the seventh, which then became the happiest and most important day of my life.

LOVING A PET

My husband is a birder, formerly known as a bird watcher. He has an enviable list of over 760 North American species, which he's recorded over many years. There was a time in our marriage when I thought of this sport as an expensive obsession; a rarity would be reported in some remote corner of a garbage landfill in, say, Galveston, Texas, and John would take off, binoculars in hand. When rare-bird alerts were posted on the Internet, John's trips became more frequent. I never resented his passion. Birding, after all, is a noble sport since top scorers don't get any money, life lists are self-monitored via the honor system, and nothing gets killed. Plus, when I added up the cost of all those flights, birding was still cheaper and less time consuming than golf. But it was John's love of his backyard birds that made me think differently about these tiny-brained creatures. We'd watch the amorous cardinal snuggle with his bride, the sassy red-winged blackbird bully her way into the bird feeder, the tiny goldfinch sing for his supper. They are John's "pets," and he loves them.

We love animals because we sometimes see similarities between our behavior and theirs, and we are fascinated by the unfiltered emotions and skills that animals and pets display. Biologist Marc Bekoff, author of *Animals at Play*, told a touching story in *New Scientist* magazine of two Jack Russell terriers, Bill and Ben, who were found on the street, filthy and cowering. Ben had been stabbed in both of his eyes, and Bill would bark at anyone who approached. They were rescued and rehabilitated, and when the blind Ben was finally reunited with his pal in an animal shelter, Bill "walked him around the yard until he was familiar with the lie of the land. Since then Bill has acted as Ben's guide dog, nudging and tugging to help him get around."

B iologists and zoologists have recorded stories of alpha male aggression, jealousy and spite, grief and gratitude. At *Reader's Digest*, animal stories were always top rated by readers. There was the dog adopted by soldiers in Iraq and smuggled back into the U.S.; the hero pet who saved his owner's life when she slipped off a ledge while jogging; the humpback whale who, tangled in a mess of crab traps and finally freed by divers, "thanked" her rescuers by nudging them and swimming with them for ten minutes. But the story that touched all of our hearts took place at the Elephant Sanctuary, where neglected and abused circus elephants find refuge from torture and confinement. One elephant, Jenny, had been tied up for twenty-three hours a day as the troupe traveled from city to city. After she became crippled, the circus dumped her and she wound up at the sanctuary. Jenny was morose until one day she spotted Shirley, an elephant who twenty-three years earlier had been a surrogate mother to Jenny for a few weeks when Jenny was a calf. The reunion was instant, marked by trumpeting and celebratory bumping. Shirley and Jenny were inseparable until Jenny's leg injury rendered her near death. Shirley and the other elephants stood vigil for days, stroking Jenny until she died. This was palliative care, a loving and dignified ending to a tortured life.

The American Society for the Prevention of Cruelty to Animals surveyed thousands of veterinarians to find out the **most popular pet names**. Here are the top seven:

1. **MAX**
2. **SAM**
3. **LADY**
4. **BEAR**
5. **SMOKEY**
6. **SHADOW**
7. **KITTY**

We spend over $40 billion a year grooming, pampering, feeding, inoculating, and accessorizing our pets. We have designated "pet friendly" cities, restaurants, hotels, even offices. When *The New York Times* published a story about the high cost of veterinary care (nearly $10 billion), they asked readers what lengths they've gone to care for their pets. The comments included: "I don't care if I eat dinner tonight or any other night, but I will go to the ends of the earth to make sure that my two basset hounds eat well." Or "My 13-year-old cat is my closest and dearest companion."

In Britain, students have asked to bring their pets with them to lectures as "support dogs." According to the U.K.'s TimesOnline, both the University of Sussex and Canterbury Christ Church University have allowed students who say they need emotional support to bring pets to their classrooms. Also in Britain, nearly half of all pet owners allow their four-legged friends to sleep with them. In the U.S., that number is about 47 percent, according to the American Pet Products Association.

Animals are guileless, foxes and jackals notwithstanding. Their primitive behavior is often a welcome reminder of what it takes to survive as we try to navigate our world. We're also conditioned from birth to view animals as friends: we sleep with teddy bears, bathe with rubber ducks; are entertained by bears (Winnie, Paddington), elephants (Babar, Dumbo), bugs (Charlotte, the Hungry Caterpillar), horses (Black Beauty, Misty), primates (Curious George), rabbits (Peter, the Runaway Bunny), and dogs (Lassie, Spot).

It's no wonder that animal images reach our emotions and spur us to action. A polar bear perched precariously on a slab of ice can galvanize a movement around the melting polar ice cap. A bald eagle soaring in the sky can prompt a patriotic outburst of "God Bless America." After the 2008 presidential election, one of the most dramatic in our history, more than 2,000 news stories recapped President Obama's victory speech. But the story that really had legs was the "dog story." Over 5,000 reports mentioned the puppy that was promised to the Obama daughters. And that story had a longer tail than the speech.

Seven Degrees of Separation

Kevin Bacon was right—almost. In August of 2008, Microsoft proved the "small world theory" that any two strangers on earth are separated by just a few degrees. They analyzed 30 billion electronic conversations among 180 million people from around the world and found that distance to be 6.6 degrees. We round this up after .5, so the new number is 7.

SELF

According to the *Internet Encyclopedia of Philosophy*, "The first condition for the highest form of Aristotelian love is that a man loves himself. Without an egoistic basis, he cannot extend sympathy and affection to others. Such self-love is not hedonistic, or glorified, depending on the pursuit of immediate pleasures or the adulation of the crowd, it is instead a reflection of his pursuit of the noble and virtuous, which culminate in the pursuit of the reflective life." If you can't "love" yourself you can't love others, according to both psychologists and theologians—an unlikely combination. Jesus said it this way: "Thou shalt love thy neighbor as thyself." And Aristotle said that the good man should be a lover of self in order to enrich himself and society by doing virtuous acts.

People who can't love themselves by these standards are more likely to be depressed, envious, and lacking in self-esteem. Their emotional lens is so clouded by their own problems and perceived shortcomings that they spend most of their waking time focused on themselves. Thomas Aquinas, in his essay on ethics, framed the concept this way: "There are two things in man, his spiritual nature and his bodily nature. A man is said to love himself, when he loves his spiritual nature. And in this way a man ought to love himself, after God, more than any other person. For God is loved as the principle of goodness, on which the love of charity is founded; man loves himself in charity inasmuch as he is a partaker in this goodness."

GOD

I f God did not exist, it would be necessary to invent him," Voltaire said. He was probably right. Researchers at the University of Oxford are spending $4 million to study why people believe in God. A team of anthropologists, theologians, philosophers, and other academics will spend three years investigating whether humans are either genetically or culturally programmed to believe in a higher being.

Roger Trigg, acting director of the Ian Ramsey Centre, told the Associated Press that anthropological and philosophical research suggests that faith in God is a universal human impulse found in most cultures around the world, even though it has been waning in Britain and parts of Europe. "There are a lot of issues. What is it that is innate in human nature to believe in God, whether it is gods or something superhuman or supernatural?" he asked. "One implication that comes from this is that religion is the default position, and atheism is perhaps more in need of explanation."

Here are **seven reasons people believe in God** that do not spring from cosmology, teleology, ontology, history, or Oxford University:

❶ Believers don't want all of life to be rational. They need unexplained phenomena in order to take chances or find ways to heal after experiencing tragedy or loss. The ultimate unexplained phenomenon is God.

❷ Belief in God generates a sense of awe. The idea of God humbles believers and helps them see their place in the world. This sense of awe has also been described by astronauts who venture into outer space.

❸ Believers feel connected by a shared faith in God. These connections create communities and a common ethical culture.

❹ Believers can become reconciled to death, since many look forward to the afterlife.

❺ Believers see God as necessary to ground society in order to have a rock-solid basis for a moral value system.

❻ Believers are comforted by God because it's appealing to have someone in charge.

❼ Believers feel that without God, life would have no purpose or meaning.

Most scientists would view these seven reasons as the result of a weak mind or character. Only 7 percent of all scientists believe in God, an increase in disbelief of 37 percent from 1914 to 1998.

Belief in Personal God	1914	1933	1998
Personal belief	27.7	15	7
Personal disbelief	52.7	68	72.2
Doubt or agnosticism	20.9	17	20.8

Some scientists and many others also believe that the irrational belief in God has fueled and will continue to fuel extremism among the world's religions, will continue to undermine humanity as the solution to life's problems, and will continue to pit people against one another rather than uniting them.

The clash between religion and science has not escaped the scientists, philosophers, writers, and artists who gather annually at the TED Conference in California. The roster of attendees and speakers are society's "fat brains," people who discovered the double helix, invented virtual reality, been President of the United States, designed a museum in Bilbao, Spain, led the Chinese student protest at Tiananmen Square, and created a search engine whose name has become a verb.

Recently, Daniel Dennett, a professor at Tufts and author of *Breaking the Spell*, took on Rick Warren and his Purpose-Driven Life. But it was the atheist Richard Dawkins who brought the argument into focus a few years before. The evolutionary biologist and author of *The God Delusion* denounced intelligent design, a code word, he said, for creationism. Dawkins said that the nearly 30 million American atheists are the second largest group in the country, outnumbering all groups except for Christians. He cited data showing inverse connection between people who believed in God and intelligence. "We've reached a truly remarkable situation, a grotesque mismatch between the American intelligentsia and the American electorate. A philosophical opinion about the nature of the universe which is held by the vast majority of top American scientists is so abhorrent to the American electorate that no candidate for popular election dare affirm it in public. This means that high office in the greatest country in the world is barred to the very people best qualified to hold it—the intelligentsia—unless they're prepared to lie about their beliefs."

Then came the fireworks, not from the audience, but from Deepak Chopra, who was also on the program that day. Chopra is an M.D. and Hindu spiritualist who has popularized Eastern philosophy and healing techniques. He's a favorite on *Oprah*, and he makes a fortune from his books, his lectures, and the Chopra Center. Chopra accused Dawkins of being a scientific bully, arrogant at the extreme. He said that believing in a spiritual being did not undermine intelligence but rather enhanced it, since it required an open mind to believe in God.

What happened at TED didn't stay at TED. The Dawkins-Chopra fight continued on for years. Chopra took the offense in 2006 in a lengthy critique of Dawkins and in his six-part series called "Debunking the God Delusion," which appeared on Beliefnet. The next year, Dawkins struck back with a two-part documentary called "The Enemies of Reason." Chopra is painted as a superstitious fake, an irrational terrorist who sells snake oil to a gullible public. A clip of that interview is still posted on YouTube.

What I love about this argument from two very smart people is that each of them alludes to finding awe and wonder in the world. Whether it's God, science, or both, the wonder of the cosmos or the ingenuity of nanotechnology, the randomness of a hole in one, or a missed smash at the net, the ability to seek and find a larger truth is what compels us. People who believe in God truly love God. People who believe in man do the same. Sometimes, people can do both.

At beliefnet.com, where religion, spirituality, and pragmatic strategies for everyday living are woven into a crazy quilt of inspiration, an application called Belief-O-Matic promises to match you with the perfect faith—or none at all—if you answer twenty questions about your concept of God, the afterlife, human nature, and more. The first question is key, and, naturally, it has seven choices:

Q. What is the number and nature of the deity (God, gods, higher power)? Choose one.

❶ Only one God—a corporeal spirit (has a body), supreme, personal God Almighty, the Creator.

❷ Only one God—an incorporeal (no body) spirit, supreme, personal God Almighty, the Creator.

❸ Multiple personal gods (or goddesses) regarded as facets of one God, and/or as separate gods.

❹ The supreme force is the impersonal Ultimate Reality (or life force, ultimate truth, cosmic order, absolute bliss, universal soul), which resides within and/or beyond all.

❺ The supreme existence is both the eternal, impersonal, formless Ultimate Reality, and personal God (or gods).

❻ No God or supreme force. Or not sure. Or not important.

❼ None of the above.

&

Seven Lies Men Tell Women

❶ "Me? I graduated top of my class."

❷ "Of course I like your friends."

❸ "Honey, you're the best" (referring to sexual performance).

❹ "No, I can't call you. I don't even know where I'll be."

❺ "That dress isn't too tight. It looks great!"

❻ "They're downsizing at work. But don't worry. They won't get me."

❼ "Sure, I'll mow the lawn—as soon as this crick in my back goes away."

—From rd.com

GIRAFFIC

Most mammals, including humans, have
7 neck bones. So do giraffes. But each vertebra in
these tall blondes' necks is 10 inches.
—Sources: Zooplace.com; How Stuff Works

{ CHAPTER 4 }

Learning

You can know the name of a bird in all the languages of the world, but when you're finished, you'll know absolutely nothing whatever about the bird.... So let's look at the bird and see what it's doing—that's what counts. I learned very early the difference between knowing the name of something and knowing something.
—Richard Feynman (1918–1988)

F inding Nemo, *50 First Dates,* and *Memento* are but a few of the popular movies where the plot hinges on short-term memory loss. A BBC documentary series focused on Clive Wearing, a musicologist who had suffered a devastating case of encephalitis resulting in anterograde amnesia. He could not retain information in his working memory and convert that information to long-term memory. He became known as the man with the seven-second memory. Clive was, however, able to remember his wife, Deborah, and his music. When he sat at the piano, he could play intricate pieces—beautifully. In his book *Musicophilia,* Oliver Sacks wrote of Clive, "In some ways, he is not anywhere at all; he has dropped out of space and time altogether. He no longer has any inner narrative; he is not leading a life in the sense that the rest of us do. And yet one has only to see him at the keyboard or with Deborah to feel that, at such times, he is himself again and wholly alive."

Imagine if you were the victim of memory loss, just like Andrew Engel, a top high school student who, in his first year of college, found that he couldn't remember anything he had learned. Not a name, not a paragraph he had read, not even how to get to his class. A brain tumor was the culprit, compromising both his learning ability and his height— the tumor had damaged Andrew's pituitary gland, which secretes growth hormone. Andrew was an identical twin until he stopped growing at the height of five feet eight inches. Then people could finally tell him and his brother apart. His only hope of survival was a risky operation that could destroy whatever was left of his short-term memory. Short-term or working memory function is like a temporary holding bin that transfers important memories into long-term storage, but Andrew was unable to make the transfer.

In 2000, neuroscientist Joe Z. Tsien, then at Princeton, and his colleagues discovered that the brain actually replays events in order to create memories. These replays reinforce the cellular connections in our brains that form those memories. (That may be why it's hard to recall the lyrics of a song if you start in the middle.) There are other factors, from proteins to genetics, that affect memory, but the key seems to be reliving the moment.

Andrew's challenge was to create those cellular connections even though he had a broken feeder cable in his brain. Yet he was determined to graduate from college and get his degree. But how? Andrew had severe amnestic syndrome and was unable to retain new information for more than about sixty seconds. Like invisible ink, words, numbers, and images would start out clearly and then fade away. Clinical neuropsychologist

Dr. David Schretlen and his postdoctoral fellow Dr. Dustin Gordon of the Johns Hopkins Department of Psychiatry and Behavioral Sciences agreed to tailor a program of cognitive retraining exercises to Andrew's impairment. The goal was to enable Andrew to bypass the usual neural mechanisms required for memory formation and force new information directly into long-term memory. Andrew capitalized on his prodigious intellect, using mnemonic devices to "tag" material for memory storage and rehearsing information dozens of times.

For the next twelve years as a college student, Andrew immersed himself in repetition and rote procedures. He repeated numbers and words, reread passages, rewrote and retyped notes. He was always

---

The Seven-Day Get Smarter Guide

When the BBC decided to test learning theory, they found that making simple changes can boost brain power by as much as 40 percent. The tests were conducted by British researchers for the network's "Get Smarter in a Week" program. The following seven-day guide is a distillation of tactics by Britain's *Guardian* newspaper:

SATURDAY
Brush your teeth with your "wrong" hand and take a shower with your eyes closed.

SUNDAY
Do the crossword or Sudoku puzzle in your Sunday paper and take a brisk walk.

MONDAY
Have oily fish for dinner, and either cycle, walk, or take the bus into work.

TUESDAY
Select unfamiliar words from the dictionary and work them into conversations.

WEDNESDAY
Go to yoga, Pilates, or a meditation class, and talk to someone you don't know.

THURSDAY
Take a different route to work; watch *Countdown* or *Brainteaser*.

FRIDAY
Avoid caffeine or alcohol; memorize your shopping list.

studying, and he never quit. It worked. He had created the necessary permanent long-term memory connections that would allow him to function at a high level. He graduated from the University of Maryland, Baltimore County, in 2007 with a 4.0 grade point average and a degree in health administration and policy. Andrew had learned how to learn. And even though he still cannot transfer even a seven-digit phone number from working memory into long-term storage with ordinary exposure, he succeeded where fully functional people often fail. As Schretlen observed, "Andrew developed a laser focus, an unshakeable ability to pay attention, and a level of persistence that very few people can muster."

He'll have to maintain that focus for the rest of his life. "When I saw him for a follow-up consultation earlier this year," Schretlen said, "he had been working at a job for six months, and he was still using a GPS to drive to work in the morning because he couldn't remember how to get there! At the same time, he clearly had acquired a great deal of new knowledge about the field he studied at the University of Maryland. I think that, ultimately, his accomplishment is a testament to Andrew's personal drive more than it is to any treatment we provided."

Attention and focus are in short supply these days. Jakob Nielsen, an Internet usability specialist who targets information pollution, knows some of the reasons why. His observations make good sense, although most of us haven't thought twice about the unnecessary sights and sounds that assault us every day. Nielsen noticed that "At San Jose Airport, when you board the shuttle bus from the terminal to the parking lot you hear the message: 'Welcome to San Jose International Airport.' Since you've just flown into San

Jose, this information is hardly enlightening. Better to say something like 'Welcome. This bus goes to the Orange long-term parking lot.'" And he rails, as we all do, against the idiots who are in the warning labels industry. "In the United States, for example, you can't buy a lawnmower without a label saying that you're not supposed to mow your feet," Nielsen says. But he saves his real ammunition for the Internet. He cautions Internet editors and writers to cut their verbiage to the basics so that users get more relevant content, and he says that spam isn't simply unsolicited e-mail, it's "attention theft."

In an essay in *ACM Queue*, Nielsen claimed that "a one-minute interruption can easily cost a knowledge worker (that would include students) 10 to 15 minutes of lost productivity due to the time needed to reestablish mental context and reenter the flow state." It's gotten so bad that they've turned off Internet access in classrooms at the

---

Class Trip

The "History of the World in Seven Minutes" is a flash video that's both entertaining and educational. The creators' website states, "'World History for Us All' is a national collaboration of K–12 teachers, collegiate instructors, and educational technology specialists. It is a project of San Diego State University in cooperation with the National Center for History in the Schools at UCLA." As a curriculum guide, they suggest exploring seven key themes:

1. Patterns of Population
2. Economic Networks and Exchange
3. Uses and Abuses of Power
4. Haves and Have-Nots
5. Expressing Identity
6. Science, Technology, and the Environment
7. Spiritual Life and Moral Codes

University of Chicago Law School. Dean Saul Levmore said in an e-mail to his students, "We have a growing problem in the form of the distractions presented by Internet surfing in the classroom." Levmore warned that "class has come to consist of some listening but also plenty of e-mailing, shopping, news browsing, and gossip-site visiting."

If, like a fantasy computer, the human brain had an exabyte of long-term memory storage and unlimited random-access memory to fulfill our short-term memory needs, we probably wouldn't have a problem. Until someone figures out how to expand certain areas of brain capacity, we're stuck with the same limitations that George Miller and other cognitive scientists uncovered, including our ability to store just seven pieces of independent information in short-term memory. That's too bad, given the explosion in knowledge and information. Here's one frequently cited statistic: In 1900, there were 9,000 scientific articles published; by 1950 that number jumped to 90,000; and in 2000, a whopping 900,000 were published.

It's no wonder that digital guru Nicholas Carr's cover story in the *Atlantic*, "Is Google Making Us Stupid?" was a topic of conversation in the summer of 2008. He describes his own daily seduction into the web of virtual information and how millions, nay, billions, are experiencing similar disjointed mental hopscotching. He cites Maryanne Wolf, a developmental psychologist at Tufts, who believes that reading on the Internet makes us "decoders" of information rather than interpreters of deep meaning. She says that reading without distraction, not a natural or instinctive skill, is what allows us to make the kind of rich, intelligent connections that define great thinkers, leaders, and inventors.

A spate of other articles and blogs on reading and stupidity emerged around the same time. Michael Agger had a piece on slate.com called "Lazy Eyes: How We Read Online." It starts, "You're probably going to read this. It's a short paragraph at the top of the page. It's surrounded by white space. It's in small type. **To really get your attention, I should write like this:**

1. Bulleted list

2. Occasional use of **bold** to prevent skimming

3. Short sentence fragments

4. Explanatory subheads

5. No puns

6. Did I mention lists?

7. (I'd add a seventh, of course: pictures.)

To round out the summer fun, *The New York Times* weighed in with a somewhat mislabeled story about high school kids and reading. "Literacy Debate: Online, R U Really Reading?" by Motoko Rich had less to do with the shorthand of text messaging than with books versus reading on the Internet. The piece covers much of the same ground as Carr and Agger, but it leaves the door open in terms of judging the role the Internet has on intelligence and learning. Others are not hedging their bets, especially Mark Bauerlein, an English professor at Emory University and author of *The Dumbest Generation: How the Digital Age Stupefies Young Americans and Jeopardizes Our Future; Or, Don't Trust Anyone Under 30*. He claims that nothing less than the future of the country is at stake: "The technology that was supposed to make young adults more astute, diversify their tastes, and improve their minds had the opposite effect.... They cannot explain basic scientific methods, recount fundamental facts of American history, or name any of their local political representatives." There are lots of arguments on the other side, of course, but almost everyone agrees that distractions and the "blip culture" are having a profound effect on attention. And loss of attention can do more than undermine learning—it can endanger your life.

In 2006, a study by the National Highway Traffic Safety Administration and Virgina Tech reported that the leading factor in most crashes and near-crashes (80 percent of crashes and 65 percent of near-crashes) was driver inattention within three seconds before the event. Talking on a cell phone, eating lunch while driving, applying makeup while driving, fidgeting with CDs or iPods, and especially sending text messages are among the growing list of distractions reported. After a five-car pileup on Interstate 5 caused by a man using a handheld computer, the *Seattle Times* asked its readers to reveal their high-risk behavior while driving. Aside from the X-rated lovers, the guitar player, and the laundry-folder, the most bizarre confession was the woman who makes coleslaw while driving. "It's my signature dish to take to picnics," she explained, "and I'm always running late." She's a lot more responsible than you might think because she buys the pre-shredded cabbage, waits for a stoplight or "a lot of room between me and the car in front," and then assembles the dish. Even more chilling, one of the worst train disasters in U.S. history was likely caused by an engineer texting two fourteen-year-old boys moments before the crash that killed him along with 25 others and injured 130 more.

If the wiring in our brains is really changing as a result of the blip culture, we're in for real trouble because the stakes get even higher when you consider attention deficits among airplane pilots, soldiers, and surgeons. "Attention-Situation Awareness (A-SA) Model of Pilot Error," a 2005 technical report prepared for NASA Ames Research Center, focused on "errors of situation awareness, with some particular emphasis given to those errors related to attention allocation." One hopeful sign: neither

---

&

Paper Chase

The Rhind papyrus is an ancient Egyptian document written around 1650 B.C. It's filled with mathematical problems and puzzles. Here's one:

Seven houses contain seven cats. Each cat kills seven mice. Each mouse had eaten seven ears of grain. Each ear of grain would have produced seven hekats of wheat. What is the total of all of these?

Sound familiar? It should because of this famous riddle:

As I was going to St. Ives
I met a man with seven wives
Each wife had seven sacks
Each sack had seven cats
Each cat had seven kits
Kits, cats, sacks, wives
How many were going to St. Ives?

The pure answer is actually one—the narrator. But if the people and things he met along the way were also going to St. Ives, you might think that the answer were 2,403 (if you added the man and the narrator). But the real answer is 2,802.

- Narrator: 1
- Other man: 1
- Wives: 7
- Sacks: 49 (7 wives × 7 sacks/wife)
- Adult cats: 343 (49 sacks × 7 cats/sack)
- Kittens: 2,401 (343 cats × 7 kittens/cat)

Airbus nor Boeing have added CD changers, iPod connections, video games, or text messaging to the control panels of their jets. Dr. Gary Small, director of UCLA's Memory and Aging Research Center at the Semel Institute for Neuroscience and Human Behavior, says the human brain is malleable and changes with its environment, a term known as neuroplasticity. He calls young people who have grown up with technology "digital natives" and everyone else "digital immigrants." Functional magnetic resonance imaging (fMRI) showed that the "immigrants" could rewire their brains by learning how to master Internet search and other operations. The good news: We're adaptable. The bad news: We may be learning how to think one paragraph at a time.

E ven Nick Carr admits that his brain has changed. "Over the past few years I've had an uncomfortable sense that someone, or something, has been tinkering with my brain, remapping the neural circuitry, reprogramming the memory. My mind isn't going—so far as I can tell—but it's changing. I'm not thinking the way I used to think. I can feel it most strongly when I'm reading. Immersing myself in a book or a lengthy article used to be easy. My mind would get caught up in the narrative or the turns of the argument, and I'd spend hours strolling

---

Significant Seven

Amazon.com has a best books of the month page where they discount best-sellers. But that's not all. "In addition to our regular Significant Seven picks, you can find seven more picks on the side (since we always have more books we want to share), our favorite new paperbacks, and up-to-date lists of the bestselling books of the month." They also feature seven categories with more recommendations: Biographies and Memoirs; Cooking, Food, and Wine; History; Literature and Fiction; Mystery and Thrillers; Nonfiction; Science and Nature.

through long stretches of prose. That's rarely the case anymore. Now my concentration often starts to drift after two or three pages. I get fidgety, lose the thread, begin looking for something else to do. I feel as if I'm always dragging my wayward brain back to the text. The deep reading that used to come naturally has become a struggle."

Technology and multitasking aren't the only monsters lurking in the closet. Emotions and biology play their part as well. A few years ago, I was invited to be "principal for a day" at my old grammar school in Brooklyn, New York. I prepared for my assignment by digging through the box of school memorabilia my mother had saved, in spite of the lack of storage space in her cramped apartment. There were annual class photos, the most peculiar of which had been taken in the sixth grade. I was tall for my age, so it looked like I had been held back two years even though I was one of the youngest in the class. There was the high school yearbook, the pins and rings. And, of course, there were the report cards. At first glance, it looked like I had breezed through school with high marks and high honors. Then I came across my first seventh-grade report card, and it all came flooding back in a wave of nausea.

There were plenty of clues as to what had gone wrong: thirty-five days playing hooky, for one; unsatisfactory in "effort," for another; and comments from teachers about my loss of focus for another. "Jackie could be one of my best students if she paid more attention in class." I was twelve years old, in a new middle school, and I was into learning. Learning how to smoke, hang out with boys, how to fool my parents. I was not alone. Ask the average teacher what it's like to teach middle school and they'll tell you it can be the most challenging—and potentially the most rewarding—experience.

The challenge is obvious in terms of discipline. But the rewards are even more dramatic because of new brain research. Until recently, scientists concluded that the twelve-year-old, seventh-grade brain was a fait accompli. Puberty marked the passage of childhood to adulthood, and the metamorphosis was complete. We celebrate this passage with religious ceremonies and expect these new young "men and women" to behave with newfound maturity. In the past, we put these adolescents to work as apprentices, interns, and other slave labor, and even betrothed them in arranged marriages. But thanks to the work of Dr. Jay Giedd, chief of brain imaging in the child psychiatry branch at the National Institute of Mental Health, and associates from a variety of institutions, we now know that although the brain is fully grown at about age twelve, it's not fully formed.

Giedd says that this ripe, robust seventh-grade brain is ready for pruning. The idea is that maturation peels away the unwanted or unused connections while reinforcing those that ultimately will declare one's identity or enable one's natural talent or curiosity. So if a seventh-grader never reads books, never plays an instrument, or never interacts socially with others, he may be peeling away the opportunity to learn certain skills. In a PBS *Frontline* special, "Inside the Teenage Brain," Giedd said, "The pruning-down phase is perhaps even more interesting, because our leading hypothesis for that is the 'Use it or lose it' principle. Those cells and connections that are used will survive and flourish. Those cells and connections that are not used will wither and die. So if a teen is doing music or sports or academics, those are the cells and connections that will be hard-wired. If they're lying on the couch or playing video games or MTV, those are the cells and connections that are going [to] survive."

Hep, Hep, Hooray

The Heptarchy, from the Greek for "seven realms," is the name
applied by historians to the period (500–850 A.D.) in English history after
the Anglo-Saxon conquest of England. It's derived from the seven
kingdoms of Northumbria, Mercia, East Anglia, Essex, Kent, Sussex,
and Wessex, which eventually merged to become the Kingdom of
England during the early tenth century.

Brain sculpting promotes maturity and new abilities to organize, manage time, and prepare for life on one's own. Perhaps that's why at age twenty-one, most people are ready to enter the adult world. Giedd began his studies focused on ADD, attention deficit disorder—a perfect orientation for understanding the distractions of puberty—and soon learned that the twelve-year-old brain was a rich source of untapped data. This is a brain that has not yet decided on its true identity, has not committed to its field of expertise, has not experienced many of the emotions that will shape it, has not felt the power of its own physical ability. It's a brain that's vulnerable to the different influences that will shape its destiny.

Lesson Learned

Jerry Tarde has been the chief editor of Golf Digest *since 1984. He's also the chairman and editorial director of Condé Nast's Golf Digest Publications, which includes* Golf World, Golf Digest Index, Golfdigest.com, *and more than thirty international affiliates.*

My dad was not much of a sports fan. I remember him taking me to Connie Mack Stadium to see my first baseball game, but the memory is of paying some hoodlums on the street two bits to watch our black-and-white 1960 Chevy Impala. He disdained the Eagles and thought the Flyers were as fake as the wrestlers at the Philadelphia Arena. He thought Joe Louis was the best heavyweight fighter who ever lived, but the sporting hero in our house was, of all things, a golfer who studied literature at Harvard and law at Emory, a son of the South, who was so unlike my father in all things that I struggled to understand their connection.

Dad was still a boy when Bobby Jones came to play in the 1930 U.S.

M y seventh-grade report cards did not reflect what I really learned that year. I didn't know it then, of course, but I was developing two of the seven kinds of intelligence that Howard Gardner, the John H. and Elisabeth A. Hobbs Professor of Cognition and Education at the Harvard Graduate School of Education, has etched into the lexicon:

❶ LINGUISTIC INTELLIGENCE: as in a poet

❷ LOGICAL-MATHEMATICAL INTELLIGENCE: as in a scientist

❸ MUSICAL INTELLIGENCE: as in a composer

❹ SPATIAL INTELLIGENCE: as in a sculptor or airplane pilot

Amateur Championship at Merion, outside Philadelphia. Jones had already won the U.S. Open, British Open, and British Amateur that year. My father was hired as a runner for Western Union. He leapfrogged the holes, took down the scores, and ran back to the clubhouse where the results were telegraphed to the nation's newspapers. When Jones beat Gene Homans in the final, it was to win the Grand Slam—a feat never before or since accomplished, called at the time "the Impregnable Quadrilateral."

At age twenty-eight, at the peak of his abilities, Jones retired, never to play serious golf again. It culminated in what my father thought—and who am I to disagree—was the most remarkable and symmetrical career in sports history. Jones began playing competitive golf at fourteen, a prodigy who tore up scorecards while not winning a single major championship for seven years. Then, coming of age, he won everything and kept winning. They were known as the "Seven Lean Years" followed by the "Seven Fat Years," I heard my father say.

Dad worked in textile mills and railroad yards his whole life. When he came home at night, my mother made him change his clothes at the door, he was so covered in grime and filth. He had a lifetime of lean years so that I would know nothing but the fat. It took awhile, but the lesson wasn't lost on me.

❺ BODILY KINESTHETIC INTELLIGENCE: as in an athlete or dancer

❻ INTERPERSONAL INTELLIGENCE: as in a salesman or teacher

❼ INTRAPERSONAL INTELLIGENCE: exhibited by individuals with accurate views of themselves

As you'd expect, there's controversy about Gardner's relativistic list. Is bodily kinesthetic ability intelligence or talent? But even the brightest bulb in the pack can be an underachiever if he doesn't have the emotional intelligence to convince people that his ideas, his talent, or his ability is worth a shot. That's where psychologist and author Daniel Goleman comes in. An entire industry has been built around his 1995 book, *Emotional Intelligence*, which has been implemented and adapted in schools, business, government, and sports.

There are endless stories of brilliant executives who lost the promotion because they were too arrogant, egotistical, or downright mean to the little guys in the office. Great managers know who's managing up, and who's lousy at managing down. They know that if a person can't treat an assistant with the respect he or she deserves, she may not treat a client properly. A Harvard Business Publishing review of Adele B. Lynn's book *The EQ Interview: Finding Employees with High Emotional Intelligence* highlights this key claim by the author: that EQ accounts for 24 to 69 percent of performance success. Lynn says, "After all, what does it matter if a software engineer is ferociously hardworking if he alienates his peers?" One Australian management resource group, Genos, cites **seven successful skills of workplace EQ:**

1. **EMOTIONAL SELF-AWARENESS:** the first necessary step in developing a high EQ

2. **EMOTIONAL EXPRESSION:** revealing one's own feelings, being vulnerable

3. **EMOTIONAL AWARENESS OF OTHERS:** compassion, understanding

4. **EMOTIONAL REASONING:** using emotional information to make decisions

5. **EMOTIONAL SELF-MANAGEMENT:** coping skills, grace under pressure, being a role model

6. **EMOTIONAL MANAGEMENT OF OTHERS:** influencing others' moods, attitudes

7. **EMOTIONAL SELF-CONTROL:** resilient in the face of adversity, not volatile, having a long fuse

I suppose one could learn how to boost EQ, up to a point. But that presumes that our biology plays a limited role. That's certainly not true when it comes to seventh-graders and teens going through puberty. New research confirms what every parent of a pubescent child already knows: the adrenal sex hormones that spew estrogen and testosterone into the bloodstreams of teens affect the neurochemicals, like serotonin and oxytocin, that regulate the highs and lows of mood.

Trial by Jury

The Seventh Amendment to the United States Constitution codifies the right to jury trial in certain civil trials.

New revelations about the teen brain explain other learning phenomena. Sleep, for instance, is essential to memory and learning. Harvard Medical School researchers tested teens on their cognitive and dexterous abilities. Both were enhanced by a good night's sleep. Adults benefit as well. Those among us who like to do crossword puzzles before turning out the lights believe that the brain does more than learn while it sleeps; it actually reasons. That's why we can wake up the next morning and fill in "7 across," the very clue that stumped us the night before.

What's exciting about this new brain research is that we can finally take a holistic approach to understanding learning, talent, emotion, cognition, and physical ability. Even though we can make significant observations about the impact of sleep, hormones, and the process of brain development, none of this research undermines our individuality. None of it accounts specifically for our experiences and how those experiences shape our lives.

Now is the time for new lessons. Americans have always translated learning into achievement because we've had the freedom to do so. Just as we were challenged in our formative years as a country to overcome serious challenges, we are challenged once again—this time by the economy, global warming, terrorism, war, and the threat of worldwide pandemics. But the very technology that can distribute knowledge and expertise to the largest group of people ever can also undermine that experience by offering mind-numbing entertainment, gossip, games, and trivia. George Siemens, an associate director with the Learning Technologies Centre at the University of Manitoba, describes **seven significant trends in learning** in his essay, "Connectivism: A Learning Theory for the Digital Age":

❶ Many learners will move into a variety of different, possibly unrelated fields over the course of their lifetime.

❷ Informal learning is a significant aspect of our learning experience. Formal education no longer comprises the majority of our learning. Learning now occurs in a variety of ways—through communities of practice, personal networks, and through completion of work-related tasks.

❸ Learning is a continual process, lasting for a lifetime. Learning and work-related activities are no longer separate. In many situations, they are the same.

❹ Technology is altering (rewiring) our brains. The tools we use define and shape our thinking.

❺ The organization and the individual are both learning organisms. Increased attention to knowledge management highlights the need for a theory that attempts to explain the link between individual and organizational learning.

❻ Many of the processes previously handled by learning theories (especially in cognitive information processing) can now be off-loaded to, or supported by, technology.

❼ Know-how and know-what are being supplemented with know-where (the understanding of where to find knowledge needed).

You can hear the fireworks as people debate the merits of Siemens's observations, including the wisdom of crowds, finding information instead of knowing it, and diminishing core knowledge in favor of expeditious learning. But, once again, the critical issue is the rewiring of the brain and our ability to focus and pay attention. Filtering the cacophony of digital noise by using seven can help achieve that focus.

Learning From ABC to JXQZ

By the time a baby starts talking, he already knows hundreds of words. That's because he is able to discriminate phonetic differences, according to new research by University of Pennsylvania psychologist Daniel Swingley. So much for the blank slate. Babies may have brains like sponges, ready to sop up everything around them, but they also have preferences. Like the rest of us, they grasp the names of objects that interest them, rather than everything that's presented to them.

Babies have an intuitive grasp of math at seven months as well, based on their ability to match the change in voices with the number of people. Attentive parents are often awestruck by how quickly infants learn and grow.

Dr. T. Berry Brazelton, known as "America's pediatrician" and author of many books, including *Touchpoints: Your Child's Emotional and Behavioral Development*, once described to me, in a perfect analogy, what happens just before babies and children demonstrate a new learned skill. He said that talking, walking, learning how to control the bladder and use a toilet are dramatic leaps of learning. That's why some children disassemble before each big leap. They seem to regress, he said, and parents think they've failed. Not so. "Think of what it takes to launch a rocket into space," he said. Great energy and thrust. "For babies, it's like pulling back on a sling shot in order to launch their new ability." What a comfort that has been for parents who not only love and nurture their children but study them.

The more we understand how children learn, the more we adapt to their strengths. Joan Ganz Cooney, the visionary behind *Sesame Street* over forty years ago, has launched a new digital initiative designed to leverage emerging media to help children learn. One of the presenters at the kickoff symposium was from the Oracle Education Foundation, which has come up with a new learning equation: 3Rs X 7Cs = 21st Century Learning. Those "7 Cs" are:

1. **CRITICAL THINKING AND PROBLEM SOLVING**
2. **CREATIVITY AND INNOVATION**
3. **COLLABORATION, TEAMWORK, AND LEADERSHIP**
4. **CROSS-CULTURAL UNDERSTANDING**
5. **COMMUNICATION AND MEDIA FLUENCY**
6. **COMPUTING AND ICT FLUENCY**
7. **CAREER AND LEARNING SELF-RELIANCE**

At Penn State University, researchers created a virtual seven-year-old to study how kids learn. The cyberkid, a computer simulation, strategizes and makes choices when building a pyramid from blocks about as well as a real seven-year-old child. Dr. Frank E. Ritter, Penn State associate professor of information sciences and technology and associate professor of psychology, explains that a software program controls the cyberkid's vision and hand motions. Together they can manipulate twenty-one interlocking blocks on a computer screen. The simulation is like a real learning study of children using real blocks.

The researchers explain that building a pyramid is an ideal task for studying development because it illustrates how children's problem-solving behavior changes across ages. Changing the way the adult computer model chooses its construction strategies most closely matched the actual behavior of real seven-year-old children. The finding suggests that seven-year-olds improve more in strategy selection as they grow rather than in the number of facts they can process simultaneously or recall at one time.

Still, learning facts—names of presidents, state capitals, and the like—is an important part of our common culture. The Parent Institute offers this advice: Use the rule of seven. Divide the list into groups of no more than seven items or chunks. To plant them in your child's long-term memory takes three things: practice, practice, practice. If kids learn how to break down what may seem like overwhelming amounts of work and information, they'll likely succeed not only in school, but at other life tasks as well. Of course they'll have to maintain their focus and attention, but that mandate is true for all ages, even the oldest among us.

Doris Haddock, known as Granny D, calls herself an "old runt of a woman, who, at my tallest was five-three, but has shrunk down to five feet." At age ninety, Haddock, now a centenarian, walked across America stumping for campaign finance reform. Four years later, she became the Democratic Nominee to the U.S. Senate in New Hampshire. In one of her speeches to high school graduates in New England, she compared life to a seven-layer cake. She said that each layer is both a challenge and an opportunity and that finding and preparing for these seven layers takes an open heart and a focused mind.

If only a few of those college-bound graduates took Granny D's message to heart, they would be well equipped to face the next challenge in their lives: the Trivium and the Quadrivium, otherwise known as the Seven Liberal Arts. Although the liberal arts did not become widespread as a university curriculum until the Middle Ages, its foundation is grounded in ancient Greek and Roman history. During the Middle Ages and earlier, the *artes liberales* were designed for the elite education and training of free people. Slaves and serfs were afforded *artes iliberales*, otherwise known as vocational training. The Trivium consisted of grammar, rhetoric, and dialectic (language, oratory, and logic), preparing students for their roles as statesmen, politicians, military leaders, and philosophers. The Quadrivium (arithmetic, geometry, astronomy, and music) prepared them for their roles as inventors, composers, and scientists.

According to the *Catholic Encyclopedia*, "By the number seven the system was made popular; the Seven Arts recalled the Seven Petitions of the Lord's Prayer, the Seven Gifts of the Holy Ghost, the Seven Sacraments, the Seven Virtues, etc. The Seven Words on the Cross, the Seven Pillars of Wisdom, and the Seven Heavens might also suggest particular branches of learning. The seven liberal arts found counterparts in the seven mechanical arts; the latter included weaving, blacksmithing, war, navigation, agriculture, hunting, medicine; and the *ars theatrica*. To these were added dancing, wrestling, and driving. Even the accomplishments to be mastered by candidates for knighthood were fixed at seven: riding, tilting, fencing, wrestling, running, leaping, and spear-throwing."

Plutarch's advice on the education of children from *Moralia* is as relevant today as it was in the second century. The major shortcomings in his work are his disregard for the education of women and his acceptance of slavery as the status quo. Yet he believed in education for the masses: "Even the poor must endeavor, as well as they can, to provide the best education for their children, but, if that be impossible, then they must avail themselves of that which is within their means."

He also eschewed corporal punishment as a method of disciplining children. "Children ought to be led to honorable practices by means of encouragement and reasoning, and most certainly not by blows or ill-treatment. Praise and reproof are more helpful for the free-born than any sort of ill-usage, since the praise incites them toward what is honorable, and reproof keeps them from what is disgraceful."

I have distilled Plutarch's **seven key points of learning**, followed by excerpts from *Moralia*:

❶ *Inspire them with stories of greatness. Read to them, but stay away from celebrity gossip.* It seems to me, Plato quite properly advises nurses, even in telling stories to children, not to choose at random, lest haply their minds be filled at the outset with foolishness and corruption.

❷ *Help children choose friends with good character.* Companions of young masters should be sought out who are, first and foremost, sound in character, and distinct of speech. The proverb-makers say, and quite to the point, If you dwell with a lame man, you will learn to limp.

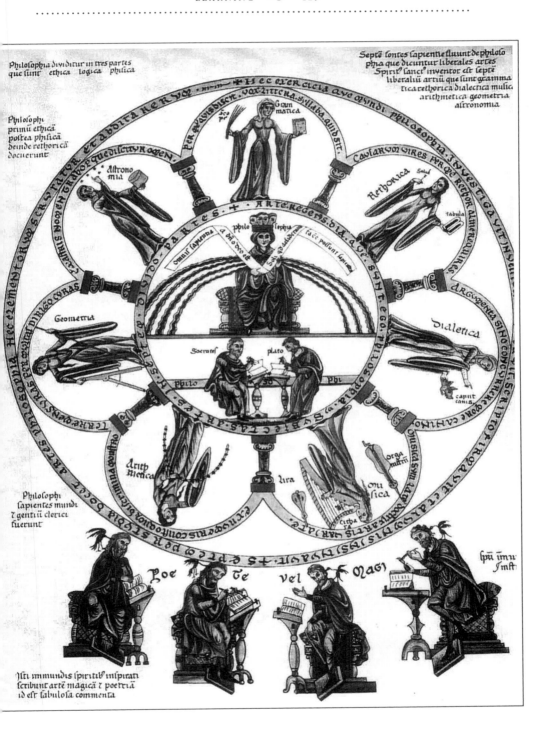

❸ *Parents and society must seek outstanding teachers who are held accountable.* Teachers must be sought for the children who are free from scandal in their lives, who are unimpeachable in their manners, and in experience the very best that may be found.

❹ *Parents and society must invest in qualified and outstanding teachers because a poorly educated society will sink itself.* Many fathers go so far in their devotion to money, that in order to avoid paying a larger fee, they select as teachers for their children men who are not worth any wage at all—looking for ignorance, which is cheap enough. Badly educated sons disdain the sane and orderly life, and throw themselves headlong into disorderly and slavish pleasures. Some of them take up with flatterers and parasites, abominable men of obscure origin, corrupters and spoilers of youth. If these men had become conversant with the higher education, they perhaps would not have allowed themselves to be dominated by such practices, and they would at least have become acquainted with the precept of Diogenes, who with coarseness of speech, but with substantial truth, advises and says, Go into any brothel to learn that there is no difference between what costs money and what costs nothing.

❺ *Ensure a common core curriculum to help forge a just and civil society.* Children should not be allowed to go without some knowledge of every branch of what is called general education; but philosophy should be honored above all else. Make philosophy the head and front of all education. For as regards the care of the body men have discovered two sciences, the medical and the gymnastic, of which the one implants health, the other sturdiness; but for the illnesses and affections of the mind philosophy alone is the remedy. For through philosophy it is possible to attain knowledge of what is honorable and what is shameful, what is just and what is unjust, how a man must bear himself in his relations with the gods, with his parents, with his elders, with strangers, with those in authority, with friends, with women, with children, with servants.

⑥ *Learn about the past in order to thrive in the future.* It is useful, or rather it is necessary, not to be indifferent about acquiring the works of earlier writers, but to make a collection of these, like a set of tools in farming. For the corresponding tool of education is the use of books, and by their means it has come to pass that we are able to study knowledge at its source.

⑦ *Learn physical discipline and fitness.* We should send the children to the trainer's and cultivate adequately this side of education with all diligence, not merely for the sake of gracefulness of body but also with an eye to strength; for sturdiness of body in childhood is the foundation of a hale old age.

The Center of Inquiry in the Liberal Arts at Wabash College assesses the impact of a liberal arts education as well as the best teaching practices. Its leaders have identified **seven elements that, when considered together, are distinctive indicators of a liberal arts education.**

❶ EFFECTIVE REASONING AND PROBLEM SOLVING

❷ INCLINATION TO INQUIRE AND LIFELONG LEARNING

❸ INTEGRATION OF LEARNING

❹ INTERCULTURAL EFFECTIVENESS

❺ LEADERSHIP

❻ MORAL REASONING

❼ WELL-BEING

THE LEARNING POWER OF SEVEN

T he seven liberal arts may have inspired other "sevens" in education. Michigan State University lists the "Seven Principles for Good Practice in Undergraduate Education," adapted from Arthur W. Chickering and Zelda F. Gamson's book. The Olin and Uris Libraries at Cornell University offer "The Seven Steps of the Research Process," and Bryn Mawr's Naomi J. Halas listed the "Seven Steps to Success in Graduate School (and Beyond)." The most dramatic of all, perhaps, is the worldwide interconnected library system, known as the Dewey Decimal Classification. They claim that "the Dewey Decimal Classification (DDC) system is constantly updated to keep pace with knowledge," and that "the editors review every part of the DDC over a seven-year cycle."

One of the consistent themes over these 2,000 years of educational philosophy is that learning is a lifelong activity. For some, changes in society and culture can be intimidating and off-putting, causing a sense of dread. For others, they are an opportunity to master a new or old discipline, to understand the world as it is, not as you remember it in your salad days. I. F. Stone, the muckraking radical journalist, studied Greek well into his seventies because he wanted to read the works of Plato and others without a translation filter. Academy Award–winning director Sidney Lumet (*Fail-Safe*, *Dog Day Afternoon*, *Network*) made the leap from film to digital imagery while in his eighties. He told an audience at the New York Film Festival in 2007, "I don't think there is one director who has ever *liked* film except as a tactile thing. It's a pain in the ass. It's cumbersome. It's rigid in its rules. And you're constantly at the mercy of the lab."

For those of us with less stellar résumés, learning new skills often means taking courses in one of the booming adult learning centers on urban campuses or taking up guitar or piano, knowing that we'll never go on world tour or be tapped for *American Idol*. The curious mind—the mind that wants to learn—will build new synapses, even in old age. Playing games like bridge and poker can also boost brain power. Can poker teach you more than how to gamble so you don't lose your shirt? A Harvard Law School professor, along with a group of his students, seems to think so. Their organization, the Global Poker Strategic Thinking Society, espouses the notion that poker can teach risk assessment, situational analysis, math, and people skills to kids from grade twelve through grad school. As a seasoned poker player, I would say this is a little like backing in. Games can be, however, good for the mind. There is a group of seven puzzles on the Internet, created by Serhiy Grabarchuk, author of *The Simple Book of Not-So-Simple Puzzles*. His website, Age of Puzzles: A Colorful Journey through Endless Patterns of Quick Wits, features this brain teaser, called Seven Stars:

Seven Stars

With three straight lines divide the Seven shown below into seven parts so that each part contains a single star.

(Answer is on page 138)

SEVEN LETTERS

My favorite game is an old standard: Scrabble. It's the perfect game, using just seven letters at each turn. It's one of the more popular applications on Facebook, because you can set up virtual games with your friends. My daughter and I play whenever we both find a few minutes. Scrabble has been around for more than sixty years, and it's likely to endure throughout this century since it's now platform agnostic. It would also take a lifetime to look at the more than 10 million Scrabble links on the Internet. Alfred Butts, who invented Scrabble when he was a jobless architect during the Depression, would have loved to see the action unfold online where millions of people compete globally. He died in 1993 at the age of ninety-three. If you use all your letters (50 points) by playing a word like *muzjiks* on your first turn, you can score 128 points. A muzjik, by the way, is a Russian peasant. If Scrabble doesn't do it for you, try a word game from the break-the-rules 1960s. It's called Oulipo, and if you don't mind destroying a beautiful poem, this game's for you. Oulipo started when a group of French mathematicians and writers invented a new system of prose and poetry. It's derived from "*Ou*voir de *litt*érature *po*tentielle," translated as the "workshop of potential literature." The prefix tells

Books of Seven

A heptalogy is a series of seven works of art. J. K. Rowling's *Harry Potter* books, C. S. Lewis's *The Chronicles of Narnia*, and Stephen King's *The Dark Tower* all qualify.

the story because this group would take a well-known poem or literary passage and replace each noun with the seventh noun that appeared after it in a dictionary. This form of reconstruction is a little like today's musical mash-ups. So, using my dictionary, the following would be my **"Oulip of the tongue"**:

❶ *I wandered lonely as a cloud* becomes
I wandered lonely as a clove.

❷ *Quoth the Raven, nevermore* becomes
Quoth the rawhide, nevermore.

❸ *Half a league, half a league, half a league onward* becomes
Half a leak onward.

❹ *April is the cruelest month* becomes
April is the cruelest moon.

❺ *But soft, what light through yonder window breaks* becomes
What light through yonder windshield breaks.

❻ *Something there is that doesn't love a wall* becomes
Something there is that doesn't love a wallet.

❼ *Apeneck Sweeney spreads his knees* becomes
Apeneck Sweeney spreads his knickers.

Still not convinced that seven is the magical number for linguists? You might look at the sales of Michael Pollan's book *In Defense of Food*. In a blog post in *The New York Times*, Tara Parker-Pope says, "The popularity of the book is due in no small part to Mr. Pollan's catchy seven-word edict: 'Eat food. Not too much. Mostly plants.'"

Here's my contribution: Play games. Fall in love. Have fun.

SEVEN WORDS

GeEorge Carlin was never accused of being a poet, although he was charged with and convicted of violating New York's obscenity laws. Carlin broke a lot of rules on television and was censored because of that. Here's what he said that got him into deep doo-doo: "There are 400,000 words in the English language, and there are seven of them that you can't say on television. What a ratio that is: 399,993 to 7. They must really be bad. They'd have to be outrageous, to be separated from a group that large. 'All of you over here, you 7. Bad words.' You know the seven, don't you? *Shit, Piss, Fuck, Cunt, Cocksucker, Motherfucker,* and *Tits,* huh? Those are the heavy seven." Carlin may not have thought of these words as bomb throwing, but many people would not only be offended, they'd be furious enough to come back with a left hook. There are seven better ways to insult someone:

❶ "He has Van Gogh's ear for music." —*Billy Wilder*

❷ "He is simply a shiver looking for a spine to run up." —*Paul Keating*

❸ "He had delusions of adequacy." —*Walter Kerr*

❹ "I didn't attend the funeral, but I sent a nice letter saying I approved of it." —*Mark Twain*

❺ "He has no enemies, but is intensely disliked by his friends." —*Oscar Wilde*

❻ "He has the attention span of a lightning bolt." —*Robert Redford*

❼ "He is a self-made man and worships his creator." —*John Bright*

Words can harm or they can heal. In Britain, James Burgess and Richard Grey have created the 7 Words Life Management Technique. From marriage to business to psychology, the following seven words, they claim, can make your life more rewarding, more successful, and more complete: *No, Hello, Thanks, Goodbye, Please, Sorry, Yes.* Or you could log on to "7 Words of Wisdom Here for You" and find **seven-word Haiku-like missives.** For example:

Hold Fast Onto

Your Moments

Of

INSIGHT

Hold the Acid Rain

Seven is "neutral" on the pH scale.
Pure water has a pH of seven. —*Wikimedia*

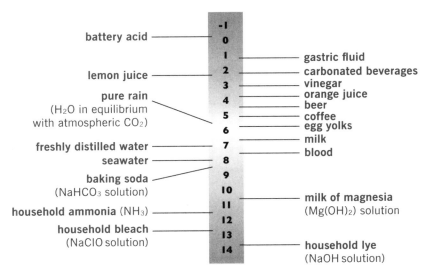

- battery acid — 0
- gastric fluid — 1
- lemon juice — 2
- carbonated beverages — 2
- vinegar — 3
- pure rain (H_2O in equilibrium with atmospheric CO_2) — 4
- orange juice — 4
- beer — 5
- coffee — 5
- egg yolks — 6
- milk — 6
- freshly distilled water — 7
- blood — 7
- seawater — 8
- baking soda (NaHCO$_3$ solution) — 9
- milk of magnesia (Mg(OH)$_2$) solution — 11
- household ammonia (NH$_3$) — 11
- household bleach (NaClO solution) — 13
- household lye (NaOH solution) — 14

After receiving her business degree at Stanford, Jacqueline Novogratz became an investment banker, but not for long. She gave up Wall Street (smart woman) when she took a trip to Rwanda and saw a child wearing a blue sweater that looked like one she had given to Goodwill. She asked to see the sweater and, sure enough, there was her name written on the label. She knew then that we're all connected, and when she saw what she was connected to—rampant poverty, violence, disease, and despair—she decided to help. But Novogratz is no bleeding heart. She's a pragmatic, feet-on-the-ground businesswoman who knows how to get things done. She started the Acumen Fund, got donations from Fortune 500 companies, and has funded over thirty-eight projects in poverty-stricken parts of Africa and Asia. She has also written a book about her work called *The Blue Sweater.* Her husband, Chris Anderson, is a perfect match. Born in Pakistan where his father was a missionary eye surgeon, Anderson never lost his sense of purpose—first as a journalist in the high-tech world, then as a man who believes that people who have good ideas to share should be heard. He gives them a platform at global TED Conferences held around the world.

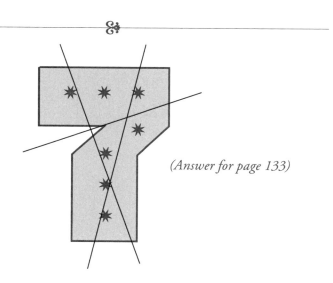

(Answer for page 133)

Under the Tuscan Sky

Jacqueline Novogratz is founder and CEO of Acumen Fund, a nonprofit global venture fund that uses entrepreneurial approaches to solve the problems of global poverty. Acumen Fund currently manages more than $30 million in investments in South Asia and East Africa, all focused on delivering affordable health care, water, housing, and energy to the poor.

I'm the eldest of seven in a big, extended Catholic immigrant Austrian-American family. My British husband grew up in Pakistan, the son of missionaries for whom a fierce devotion to Christianity was at the center of family life. Creating a wedding ceremony that would honor our respective families' religious devotion while imbuing the day with our own approach to spirituality was no mean task.

I studied the wedding traditions of many great religions, looking for patterns and truths that transcended all of them. More often than not, the number seven was at the core of organizing principles, blessings, and truths. I'd been to Jewish weddings and loved the notion of the Seven Blessings. The Seven Steps in the Hindu wedding ceremony were accompanied by the couple circling a fire. Catholics practice the Seven Sacraments, and some Muslims embrace Seven Pillars of Islam. Buddhists place seven bowls of water to symbolize the different stages of Buddhism. In each of these, we found great beauty and wisdom, and also ideas we weren't as keen on celebrating at our wedding.

We decided to accept the importance of seven as our organizing principle, a reference to the wisdom of many religions, our way of bowing to those who came before us. And we chose seven words to symbolize what we felt was most important to a successful marriage, the blessings we hoped to receive and to give to other couples in our lives.

Our loved ones stood around us in a circle on a summer day in Italy just as the sun was beginning to set. When it came time for the seven blessings, a close friend or family member would step into the circle to share a prayer or blessing or poem, their wish for us inspired by the word we gave to them. We chose simple words: love, grace, friendship, kindness, patience, commitment, and humor. Our loved ones revealed a part of themselves in the blessings they shared with us, offering wisdom from Rumi, Plato, the Bible, and their own hearts, providing everyone in that circle a single, shared prayer in seven parts.

Just as the last blessing was given and we turned to face each other as husband and wife, we heard the bells toll seven times in the seventh month on an unforgettable Tuscan evening.

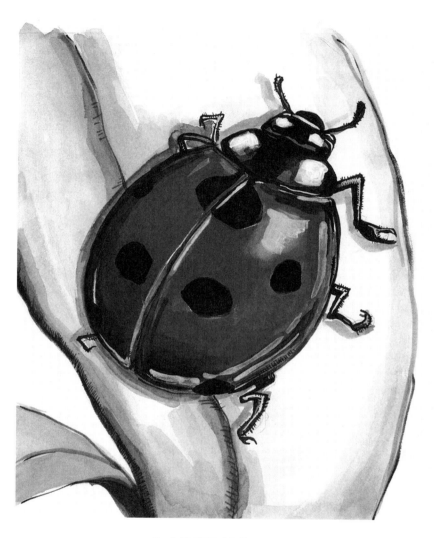

LADYBUG LUCK

*The seven-spot ladybug, or ladybird in the U.K., is a symbol of
luck, and rightly so—it eats aphids and is highly prized
by gardeners. The term* ladybird *comes from the Middle Ages,
when the creature was named after the Virgin Mary. The
seven spots of the common European variety symbolize seven joys
and seven sorrows, just like my experience in Vegas.*
—*Source: BBC*

CHAPTER 5

Winning

At the age of six I wanted to be a cook. At seven I wanted to be Napoleon. And my ambition has been growing steadily ever since.
—Salvador Dali 1904–1989

What makes a winner? Charisma and personality? Breeding and genetics? Talent and intelligence? All of the above? Or is it just plain luck? Theories come from people in almost every sector of life: scientists, lawyers, sports stars, business leaders, psychologists, educators, spiritual and religious philosophers, and, of course, politicians. And the answers often come in sevens: seven laws, steps, ways, strategies, secrets, and keys. A simple search yields *The Seven Laws of Spiritual Success*; *The Millionaire Zone: 7 Winning Steps to a Seven-Figure Fortune*; *Free Throw: 7 Steps to Success at the Free Throw Line*; *The 7 Secrets of Successful Parents*; *Exceeding Expectations: Mastering the Seven Keys to Professional Success*; *Poker: Seven Ways to Win*; *The 7 Secrets of Learning Revealed*, and over 200,000 other titles (not including this one). But the mother of them all, with over 15 million copies in print, is *The 7 Habits of Highly Effective People*. Author Stephen Covey goes to the heart of being a winner in life, no matter what you do for a living or how you measure success. He ignores the external trappings of a simple how-to formula like "dress for success" and zeroes in on character, the core element of self-improvement.

In 1989, when others were touting aspects of personality, e.g., "He's so charismatic" or "She's a popular public speaker and networker," Covey's *7 Habits* focused on intrinsic character. What Covey believed and espoused was that character can be taught, whereas other personal attributes may be genetic and unchangeable. Liars and frauds are made, not born. Heroes, too. Having courage in the face of danger is an act of will. These positive traits are evidenced in winners everywhere—from the battlefield to the baseball field.

When a baseball player makes a sign, it's rarely the sign of the cross. Unless, that is, you're Mike Piazza. He played for five different teams, retiring as a baseball legend and the best-hitting catcher of all time. Piazza didn't get to the top of the heap by cheating with steroids, and he never played "dirty," trying to derail another player. As a practicing Catholic, he found a way to win without violating the tenets of his faith. He was disciplined and kept his focus. And he identified one of the real keys to success in an interview with beliefnet.com:

"It's a game based on failure. It is a slice of life, so to speak, that life is adversity, and how you deal with adversity. In baseball, if you fail 7 out

---

Seven-Ball

It's billiards, sort of, with seven balls. To start, balls are racked in a hexagonal frame, then there's the usual break. The player then selects three pockets on one side of the table and must only use those pockets. The breaker uses the other side.

of 10 times, you're a success. It's probably not the same numbers in life. But I still feel that in life it's not so much [about] the good times. It's what you find out about yourself during the bad times. Because when the times are going good, or things are going well, everyone's on their best behavior. And it's easy to be good. But when you go through adversity, when a couple goes through frustrations, or they go through a bankruptcy, or they have bills—all these things, you see a person's true colors. And you see a person's true grace under fire, so to speak."

Confucius would have agreed with Piazza. He said, "Our greatest glory is not in never failing, but in rising every time we fail." When people say "Failure is not an option," I cringe. They may in fact need to succeed, but I don't think that message should be broadcast to young people who might become obsessive perfectionists or drop out of the game altogether in order to avoid the stigma of failure. Failure—the mistakes we make in every aspect of our lives—is how we learn to get it right the next time.

Jerry Della Femina knows about failure, not only on the playing field, but in business. He is the poster boy for rising from the ashes. When he was a newbie in the advertising business in the 1960s, everyone was predicting he'd go under. And he almost did. That's when he blew his last $3,000 on a great party for clients, media, and friends. That did it. He landed some big accounts and he was back in business. A few years later he wrote the bestseller *From Those Wonderful Folks Who Gave You Pearl Harbor*. He once said that "failure isn't terrible if you can say to yourself, hey, I know I'm gonna be successful at what I want to do someday. Failure doesn't become a big hangup then because it's only temporary. If failure is absolute, then it would be a disaster, but as long as it's only temporary you can achieve almost anything."

When I Hit Bottom in the Bottom of the Seventh Inning

Jerry Della Femina is a legendary adman and author. His books include the bestseller From Those Wonderful Folks Who Gave You Pearl Harbor *and* An Italian Grows in Brooklyn *(which was a no-seller). And now following the lead of his hero, Jimmy Breslin, Jerry Della Femina is the award-winning weekly humor columnist for the* East Hampton Independent.

When I was fourteen, I was unceremoniously thrown off a neighborhood pickup team in Brooklyn for incompetence along with a fifteen-year-old named Virgulio.

Virgulio smoked four packs of Lucky Strike cigarettes a day since he was ten and consequently was having a little trouble running wind sprints. Before Virgulio and I were sent packing, we were allowed to play a last game against a team from Bay Parkway in Brooklyn because our team only had eleven players available that day. The Bay Parkway coach was smart enough to start a young kid named Sandy Koufax, who had one pitch—a blinding fastball that you simply could not see. Koufax was also so wild that no one (himself included) had any idea where the ball was going to go once it left his hand. Occasionally, one of his errant pitches would hit and dent the metal fence backstop with a sickening clang.

The Koufax team was good and they had an 11-run lead minutes after the game started. By the 7th and last inning I was safely sitting on the bench having erotic thoughts about my earth science teacher. I led the league in erotic thoughts. Our first two batters

The idea of being a lifelong winner has little to do with having an enviable lifestyle. If you're a lifelong winner, people want to be around you because **they value you in one or a combination of these seven ways:**

❶ **A LEADER**

❷ **AN IDEA GENERATOR**

❸ **A PRODUCER**

❹ **A COMMUNICATOR**

❺ **A STRATEGIST**

❻ **A FUTURIST**

❼ **A REALIST**

struck out. Our coach looked at the bench and said, "Virgulio, take that cigarette out of your mouth and pinch hit. *You*, get onto the on-deck circle; you're batting if Virgulio gets on base." I looked around to see who he was talking to and I realized that the "you" was me.

I then did the only thing I could do under the circumstances. I started to shake. I made it to the on-deck circle and kneeled down on one knee. *Since I'm kneeling*, I thought, *I might as well pray*. I thought a quick Act of Contrition was in order since this is what Catholics do when they are about to die.

The first pitch to Virgulio was incredibly fast and right down the middle of the plate. Virgulio swung late. No, I'm being too kind; he swung so late he came close to hitting the ball that the catcher was tossing back to Koufax. "No pitcha! No pitcha!" I screamed from the on-deck circle. Under my breath I mumbled, "Oh my God, I am heartily sorry for having offended thee..."

"No pitcha! No pitcha!"

The next pitch missed Virgulio's ear by less than a millimeter. It came so fast he never had time to get out of the way. His face, which was always pale from all that smoking, turned chalky white. His reflexes, which were nonexistent, kicked in late and he threw himself to the ground while the catcher was, again, returning the ball to Koufax. Now you must understand that this was a time when there were no protective helmets. The only thing you had to protect your brain from a ninety-five-mile-an-hour pitch was your skull.

I just got to the part in the Act of Contrition where I promised to "Amend my life, Amen," when Virgulio answered my prayers by swinging at the next two wild pitches before they left Koufax's hand. The game was over. I missed my chance to say "I faced the great Sandy Koufax," but was so relieved that I contemplated carrying the shaking Virgulio off the field on my shoulders.

If you're a lifelong winner you probably exhibit some, if not all, of Covey's 7 Habits. He drew from the Greeks—Aristotle, in particular—who believed that successful societies are built on moral foundations.

A ristotle wrote that virtue was at the center of good character, flanked and often threatened by deficiency on one side, excess on the other. His often-cited virtues and vices are an instant study in character. He'd take an action or a feeling and, without benefit of an Excel spreadsheet, create a three-row comparative table. For example, self-expression is the *action*, buffoonery is *excess*, truthfulness is the *mean*, and understatement is *deficiency*.

Covey's 7 Habits	Aristotle's Ethics
BE PROACTIVE Take the initiative. Don't wait for others to define the moment, the situation, or the future.	Excellence comes about as a result of *habit*. We become just by doing just acts, temperate by doing temperate acts, brave by doing brave acts.
BEGIN WITH THE END IN MIND Set goals, visualize the end result.	*The final cause*: "The end, that for the sake of which a thing is done," e.g., good health is the end of regular fitness and good nutrition.
PUT FIRST THINGS FIRST Prioritize work, organize short-term and long-term goals.	People of good character acquire goods of moral value. They *allocate and organize* their choices against a life plan.
THINK WIN-WIN There's no point in doing a deal if you decimate or humiliate the other guy. Everyone should win.	Those who give up something for the sake of the other party cannot complain, for that is the nature of the *friendship of virtue*.
SEEK FIRST TO UNDERSTAND, THEN TO BE UNDERSTOOD	Being self-consciously *aware of oneself* entails thinking of oneself as two kinds of entities: as both the subject and object of reflective thought.
SYNERGIZE Collaborate, value teamwork.	Men address as friends their *fellow voyagers* and fellow soldiers, and those associated with them in any other kind of community.
SHARPEN THE SAW Find care and balance for mind, body, and spirit.	The liberal arts provide the leisure to make the best of *body and mind*.

Aristotle believed that all human actions are prompted by one or more of the following seven causes: chance, nature, compulsion, habit, reason, passion, and desire. And like Aristotle, Covey believed that character was built around nurturing and promoting the positive causes, controlling the dangerous ones, and understanding how, as individuals, human beings are greater than any of these "causes" or parts. Aristotle may have been the first to claim that the whole was greater than the sum of its parts, but it took about 2,300 more years for Max Wertheimer to elaborate upon the idea in Gestalt theory. He wrote, "I play a familiar melody of six tones and employ six new tones, yet you recognize the melody despite the change. There must be something more than the sum of six tones, viz. a 7th something, which is the form-quality, the Gestaltqualität, of the original six. It is this 7th factor which enabled you to recognize the melody despite its transposition."

Another proponent of this theory was Buckminster Fuller who, along with E. J. Applewhite, created *Synergetics*, a treatise that would have fascinated Aristotle, partly because of its mathematical base. "Synergy reveals a grand strategy of dealing with the whole instead of the tactics of our conventional educational system, which starts with parts and elements, adding them together locally without really understanding the whole. . . . It is dealing with the whole that makes it possible to discover the parts."

Focusing on parts as opposed to the whole is one of the reasons that the print industry is in trouble, newspapers in particular. I remember the gleeful tone in the voices of newspaper and magazine executives after the Internet bubble burst in 2000. They were congratulating themselves on not having become "road kill" on the Internet superhighway. These were the same men who had assistants both at work and at home. People who rarely answered their own phone or e-mail or shopped for books or groceries. They didn't understand why people wanted personal computers, video games, PDAs, cell phones, or digital cameras, and they didn't want to know how to use them. What they missed, of course, was that there were seven forces that were creating a new media industry. And that industry was poised to destroy them.

Ross Dawson, a business strategist and CEO of Advanced Human Technologies, issues an annual report on the future of media. In 2008, he identified the seven forces that would change the media landscape as a whole. What's striking about his list is that none of these trends is new. But when aggregated, they are a juggernaut. The whole *is* greater than the sum of its parts.

Hoochie Coochie Man

In a song written by Willie Dixon called "Hoochie Coochie Man," Muddy Waters lays out his view of the power of number seven:

On the seventh hour
On the seventh day
On the seventh month
The seven doctors say
He was born for good luck
And that you'll see
I got seven hundred dollars
Don't you mess with me
But you know I'm him
Everybody knows I'm him
Well you know I'm the hoochie coochie man
Everybody knows I'm him

SEVEN DRIVING FORCES SHAPING MEDIA

❶ INCREASING MEDIA CONSUMPTION People of all ages consume multiple media at the same time, with television, Internet, newspaper, messaging, and other media frequently overlapping. *Implications*: Average total media consumption will exceed waking hours. Most media will be consumed with partial attention. Advertising impact will decrease.

❷ FRAGMENTATION Media channels are being fragmented, even as new ones are being added. *Implications*: More media means less revenue per channel. In all except a handful of cases, production costs will need to be cut.

❸ PARTICIPATION Media activities are increasingly focused on social networks as opposed to expert authority channels. *Implications*: An infinite supply of content and increased fragmentation of attention. Pro-am (professional-amateur) content models will emerge.

❹ PERSONALIZATION Media filters are targeting advertising and information based on behaviors, location, and other profile data. *Implications*: Users' expectations for control over their media will increase. Abuse of personalized advertising will create a backlash. Some will opt out, and others will opt in if sufficient value is created.

❺ NEW REVENUE MODELS The trend is away from subscription and toward ad-supported business models. The online players with the greatest reach are advertising networks, not stand-alone sites. The promise of micropayments for content may re-emerge within a decade. *Implications*: Advertising aggregation will be central to the media landscape. Media companies will segment and unbundle ad sales and content creation.

❻ GENERATIONAL CHANGE Like music, every generation has its media favorites. For the largest generation—America's 79 million millennials—that does not include traditional television, radio, and newspapers. *Implications*: Media channels will be increasingly age-segmented. Advertisers will accelerate their shift to new media outlets.

❼ INCREASING BANDWIDTH Bandwidth will continue to increase indefinitely. It will not be too long before the majority of developed country homes receive over 100 Mbps. At the same time mobile bandwidth is soaring. *Implications*: Video on demand anywhere, anytime. Personal clouds will allow music and video collections to be accessed anywhere without local storage.

In contrast to the newspaper industry, the 2008 presidential campaign was a tale of bungling for some, undermining for others, and outstanding success for one: Barack Obama. He won the presidency in seven steps, according to journalist Howard Fineman, who spoke with David Plouffe, a campaign strategist in President Obama's inner circle. According to Fineman, "Businessmen and politicians will reverently study the campaign for years to come as a model of innovative branding and an example for digital sales strategies.... Altogether, this strategy is seven-pronged—and it's a veritable play book for political success." (I've kept Howard's headings and amended some of the text to reflect the broader ideas behind the strategy.)

❶ BE DECISIVE: "Everyone speaks his or her mind," Plouffe told Fineman, and then Barack makes the decision. There's no second-guessing, because it's better to have one strategy than to try ten in the pursuit of the perfect answer. There is no perfect answer.

② HAVE A TIGHT CIRCLE: Obama had four people he trusted around him. When voters hear that a campaign manager was fired or there was trouble in So-and-So's campaign, they lose faith in the candidate's ability to manage.

③ STICK WITH THE PLAN: Every candidate and campaign message will be criticized at one time or another. The insecure will jump and change direction, again, losing faith with voters. Remember Al Gore's alpha-male makeover?

④ SWEAT THE DETAILS: As with everything in life, the devil is in the details. It's one thing to say we're going to create an army of Internet voters, it's another to execute that promise. That takes two things: hiring the right people and managing them according to expectations. People who volunteered to make phone calls, for example, said they were given perfectly accurate, up-to-date lists that could be downloaded electronically and used efficiently. At the end of their service, they were thanked and told that they were the reason for the success of the campaign.

⑤ UNDERSTAND YOUR BRAND: Someone at the campaign was a marketing whiz. They had read the country's tea leaves and knew that people were looking not only for change but for inspiration. So symbols of a rising sun (not Japan's) were part of the Obamarama.

⑥ GO DIGITAL: These guys knew what they were doing. They created an Obama applet for the iPhone, worked with meetup.org to host local events, put up pages on Facebook and MySpace, and dominated Twitter with instant messages. Washington is still steeped in pages, assistants, interns, and a variety of old-tech ways of doing business. If you've been in D.C. for a while as a politician, you're probably still out of touch with the digital world.

⑦ USE CAUTION: Voters want action, but they want thoughtful, prudent action. They don't want someone who shoots from the hip or says the first thing that comes into his mind.

That's the Obama way.

Winning strategies are not always planned. Sometimes they're discovered—especially in business. Susan Engel, former CEO of Department 56, a wholesale distributor of decorative Christmas and holiday accessories in Minneapolis, employed a national sales force to handle a variety of products and product lines. She told me, "I learned early on that people were most comfortable selling around seven product lines, even though they had the opportunity to sell many more (and theoretically make more money on commission). It was a combination of what they were comfortable selling, but more importantly, how much information they could retain about the products they had to sell and still be effective sellers. They did well with about seven of them and were ineffective if they went above that number. So we made our incentives more general: salespeople were given revenue quotas rather than unit quotas when we learned that most of them could not handle more than seven product lines."

LUCKY NUMBER SEVEN

Planning, training, and willpower can help people become successful, but what about serendipity? Are some people simply born lucky? Or do they make their own good fortune?

Back in the late nineties, when college students were dropping out of school to start their own Web-based businesses, people thought that you had to be young and technically competent to be an Internet tycoon. Many of those companies failed, and the young CEOs were left without a dime and without a degree. Those who did succeed probably embraced the **seven keys to good luck:**

❶ **EXPECT TO WIN:** Self-fulfilling prophesies can work for or against you.

❷ **PROJECT A POSITIVE ATTITUDE ABOUT YOUR IDEAS, YOUR FUTURE:** People gravitate toward positive people.

❸ **TRUST YOUR INSTINCTS:** If the driver in front of you seems less than competent, move into another lane.

❹ **DON'T GET THROWN BY SETBACKS:** Everyone has them. Even Warren Buffett. But in the end, he believes he will win.

❺ **LEARN FROM MISTAKES AND FEEDBACK:** Failure is one step toward success.

❻ **BE A PHILOSOPHER:** Find the words to keep you motivated. Persistence pays off.

❼ **NO GUTS, NO GLORY:** Take risks. Luck comes from exposing your ideas and your plans to the world.

Like Warren Buffett, syndicated columnist Liz Smith grew up during the worst of times. Born in 1923, she and her family suffered through the Great Depression and World War II. Like many women of her era, Smith had to carve out a career in a man's world. She chose journalism, which left the door ajar for women.

Hard Times on Easy Street

Liz Smith began her career in the 1950s as a news producer for Mike Wallace at CBS Radio. Her celebrity gossip column has appeared in the **New York Daily News, Newsday,** *and the* **New York Post.** *A syndicated columnist, Smith won an Emmy for reporting in 1995. She is called "the Grand Dame of Dish," and published her biography,* **Natural Blonde,** *in 2000. She writes a column for wowowow.com.*

I was born in Fort Worth, Texas, in 1923 when it was still a little town. My father was doing a booming business as a cotton buyer and making lots of money. He was a gambler and very superstitious. He liked to shoot craps and that old Lucky Seven often came up. He was smart and could do long division in his head.

So when I was born at home at 1919 Hemphill Street, we called it "Easy Street" because it had a reputation for being "the longest street in the world." It ran right in front of our house and went on down to join the highway that led to Waco and South Texas. My father bought two houses, one for his parents six blocks away from us. He had several cars and we had a housekeeper named Dott. He kept a thoroughbred racehorse penned in the backyard and he played polo.

Where is the Lucky Seven in all of this? Well, seven years after I was born, two big things happened. I saw my first movie; it was a silent even though "talkies" had already entered Hollywood. I remember that Dott took me to the movie theater and held my hand all the way home because I was crying for the dogs that had died on the screen. This movie was *Frozen Justice*, a story about a half-Inuit Eskimo girl who was also half white. Rushing between frozen northern tundra and the bright lights of Nome, torn between nature and "civilization," her dog sled fell in a crack in the ice that then smashed together and killed her. This was quite an introduction to show business.

But even more important, this seventh year of my life also ushered in the stock market crash of 1929. Everything changed. And I got to live through the Great Depression, which really didn't entirely alleviate until about the time of World War II.

Thus, I can't say seven became a lucky number for me. But in a way it did. I became an enchanted movie fan and that sealed my fate careerwise. And I got to drop from the upper middle class right down to receiving handouts from our church so we could eat. Seeing people on the breadline. Watching my father drive himself to keep us afloat. My mother scrimping and saving and hanging out the wash. Making do. Learning to do it myself. Working, even as a kid. This was a good life lesson for someone who was at heart a happy-go-lucky hedonist.

Like Sophie Tucker, I've been rich and I've been poor and, believe me, rich is better. It is, as long as you know the difference. And the difference for me was seven years.

The number seven has always been known as a lucky number. When the calendar turned 7.7.07, the number of couples exchanging wedding vows increased dramatically. Casinos raked it in from superstitious gamblers, and thousands took the leap and started something: a new relationship, a wedding proposal, a business concept, or even a confession. Is lucky number seven just plain old superstition? Or is there more to it?

David Frankfurter, professor of religious studies and history at the University of New Hampshire, said, "In the Bible, numerology provided a very simple and clear way to indicate perfection. The sevenness of the angels, trumpets, and bowls in Revelation expresses the heavenly perfection behind all the fire and brimstone occurring on earth, as much as the seven days of creation indicate the perfection of the world around us. In the time of the finalization of the Jewish Bible, the seven vowels of the Greek alphabet became also linked to these Jewish concepts of perfection. So the 'superstitions' around seven are all good ones," he says.

In contrast to the Chinese, who revere the number eight, the Japanese have a special affinity for the number seven. Ancient Japan was founded around seven districts. Japanese Buddhists believe people are reincarnated seven times, and there are seven weeks of mourning after death. The Seven Gods of Luck in Japanese folklore are the real stars, though. They represent seven virtues: Candor, Fortune, Amiability, Popularity, Longevity, Dignity, and Magnanimity. *The Seven Samurai* is a manifestation of these virtues, and it is the title of one of the most popular and influential movies of the last century. It spawned an American clone, *The Magnificent Seven*.

ODDS ON SEVEN

Y ou can't talk about luck and numbers without hitting the gambling table and the easy chair, the latter being the essential comfort zone for sports fans. If you like dice games—from backgammon to craps—it's good to know the odds. The Wizard of Odds, a gaming website, did the calculations on a two-dice roll:

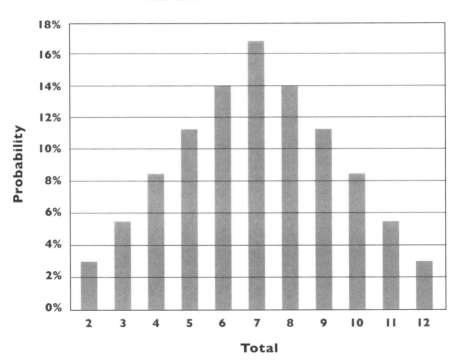

PROBABILITIES OF TWO-DICE TOTALS

Seven wins, possibly because the opposite faces of a die add up to seven. If you don't like dice games, there's always poker, a game often played with seven cards: seven-card stud; Texas hold 'em; a game I call "Brooklyn" (the wild cards are twos and one-eyed jacks, and the man with the ax [the king of diamonds], but a pair of natural sevens takes all); screw your neighbor, otherwise known as anaconda; and hundreds more. And to make a grand slam in bridge, you have to bid and make seven tricks of a suit or no trump.

CARD TRICKS

Whether at the bridge table or the poker table, when you hear "shuffle up and deal" you know you're about to embark on the exciting roller coaster of skill and chance. And it turns out that seven helps us with the "chance" part of that equation. How? The chance or luck aspect of any card game is dictated by the random, unpredictable ordering of the cards in the deck. So we shuffle again and again. But a recent mathematical theorem asserts that we need shuffle the cards only seven times to insure a thoroughly mixed-up deck.

A "perfect shuffle" of a deck of fifty-two playing cards would require cutting the deck into two piles of twenty-six cards each and then perfectly interleafing the cards of the two piles—one from one pile, one from the other, and so forth. Ironically, perfect shuffles will *not* result in a truly randomized deck of cards. In fact, if one were to perform exactly eight *perfect* shuffles, all the cards would return back to their original pre-shuffled positions in the deck.

Although we try to cut the deck in half, we rarely form two equal piles of exactly twenty-six cards. Nor do we interleaf the cards perfectly as we shuffle. It is these two defects in our shuffling abilities that, paradoxically, allow us to produce a truly mixed-up deck of cards in just seven shuffles.

In the early 1990s, mathematicians used sophisticated probability theory to prove that with fewer than five (imperfect) shuffles it is unlikely that the cards would be thoroughly mixed up. They showed that with seven shuffles the cards would be thoroughly mixed up. —*Edward B. Burger*

In sports, seven can determine the result. Take tennis, for example. The seventh game of a set is considered the critical game. At 3–3, if the server doesn't hold, it changes a tight game to one where the opponent has a commanding lead. If the server holds, there is now tremendous pressure on the opponent to hold his serve to avoid giving the other player a chance to serve for the set. Even if the score stands at 4–2, the seventh game is the swing game. There's also a seven-point tie-breaker in tennis, and the best four out of seven wins the World Series. For some, it's all about the number on your back. There are six top athletes who wore the number seven: David Beckham, Joe Theismann, Dom DiMaggio, John Elway, George Best, and Nate Archibald. But the number will always belong to the legendary seventh: Mickey Mantle.

Courting a Victory

The Chicago Seven (originally eight until Bobby Seale had his trial severed) were charged with conspiracy and inciting riots during the 1968 Democratic Convention in Chicago. They beat the conspiracy charge, but five of the seven were convicted of crossing state lines to incite a riot. They were fined and sentenced to five years in jail. Two years and nine months later, their convictions were reversed on appeal.

The Mick and a Blip in History

Jeff Greenfield is CBS News senior political correspondent; he went to his first baseball game some sixty years ago.

Mickey Mantle came to New York as a nineteen-year-old out of Commerce, Oklahoma, with neck and shoulder muscles that seemed like coiled steel beneath the number 7 on his back. He hit from both sides of the plate, and the home runs he hit were often the kind that left fans gasping; not soft fly balls that barely cleared the barriers along the foul lines—296 feet in right, 301 in left—but home runs that left the outfielders rooted to their positions in disbelief, soaring into the upper deck, or into the farthest reaches of the bleachers.

I saw many of those tape-measure jobs, but none more remarkable than the one he hit on Memorial Day, 1956—the season when he won the Triple Crown—leading the American League in batting average, runs batted in, and home runs. With two men on, Mantle hit a ball into right field that rose, rose, and kept on rising, until it struck the façade of the roof in right field, a mere eighteen inches below the top—those eighteen inches were all that kept the ball from being the only fair ball ever hit completely out of the park. Indeed, the fans out in the right-field upper deck saw the ball soar over their heads, and thought for a moment that Mantle had indeed hit one out—and the roar from that part of the field was as loud as any sound I have ever heard from any crowd, anywhere.

I always thought Mantle would forever be the most memorable "seven" of my baseball fandom; alas, that was not to be the case. In 2004, my son Dave and I went to the Stadium for Game Seven of the League Championship series. Somehow the Boston Red Sox, the team the Yankees *always* beat when the chips were down, had managed to win three straight games after falling behind 3–0. We had been given the best seats in the house, just behind home plate, and I remember jabbering to my son about the historical nature of the evening. When the Yanks fell behind 2–0, it was surely a momentary blip in the inevitability of history. Then in the second inning, with the bases loaded, Yankee pitcher Kevin Brown served up a ball to Johnny Damon that was so obviously inadequate that I yelled "Look out!" a moment before Damon hit the grand-slam home run that doomed the Yankees to the worst collapse in baseball history.

Don't tell *me* seven is a lucky number.

There are seven simple secrets of naturally lucky people, and the first is that lucky people don't believe in luck. They believe in the power of the individual. Walter Anderson is the ultimate self-made man. After he dropped out of high school to join the marines, he thought twice about his education and spent his free time studying for the GED. Anderson not only received his equivalency diploma, he went on to graduate from college and write five books, including *The Confidence Course.*

Hurl It!

It isn't a league, it's a union, which is an interesting choice of words for a sport birthed in Britain. The USA Sevens annual U.S. tournament is part of the International Rugby Board Sevens World Series. The USA Sevens is the newcomer to the World Series, which began in 1999.

When Success Isn't Enough

Walter Anderson, former chairman and CEO of Parade magazine, is a member of the U.S. National Commission on Libraries and Information Sciences. He also serves on the boards of Literacy Volunteers of America, the National Center for Family Literacy, the National Dropout Prevention Fund, Very Special Arts, the U.S. Naval Postgraduate School, and PBS.

I had an idea to teach a course about being confident, so I created "the confidence course" for the New School. I asked the administrator what would be a successful benchmark. We exceeded that number by attracting more than fifty students. The confidence course was based on my "seven steps to self-fulfillment." Being successful is different than being fulfilled. I can tell you how to be fulfilled.

Seven Steps to Self-Fulfillment

1. **SMILE.** Because no one else can do this for you.

2. **KNOW WHO IS RESPONSIBLE.** Accept personal responsibility for your behavior. When you say, "I am responsible," you can build a new life, even a new world.

3. **BELIEVE IN SOMETHING BIG.** Your life is worth a noble motive.

4. **PRACTICE TOLERANCE.** You will like yourself a lot more, and so will others.

5. **BE BRAVE.** Remember, courage is acting *with* fear, not without it. If the challenge is important to you, you're supposed to be nervous.

6. **LOVE SOMEONE.** Because you should know joy.

7. **BE AMBITIOUS.** No single effort will solve all of your problems or achieve all of your dreams. To want to be more than we are is real and normal and healthy.

PETAL PUSHERS

*The starflower (*Trientalis borealis*) has the unusual feature
of being based on sevens: seven leaves, seven petals, and
seven sepals. It grows in northern wooded areas at high elevations.
—Source: Connecticut Botanical Society*

{ CHAPTER 6 }

Life

After sleeping through a hundred million centuries we
have finally opened our eyes on a sumptuous planet, sparkling
with color, bountiful with life. Within decades we must
close our eyes again. Isn't it a noble, an enlightened way of
spending our brief time in the sun, to work at understanding
the universe and how we have come to wake up in it?
—Richard Dawkins

The number seven has a way of organizing life, from the days of the week to seven-year segments. Some take their first communion at age seven because that's considered an age of discretion; age fourteen represents the transition from childhood to adulthood in many religions and cultures—after completing a course of study, students can become full members of Ethical Culture Societies and Catholics can be confirmed; age twenty-one usually brings independence and the right to have a beer in any bar in America. But what if human beings developed at a much faster rate? At a time of great scientific advances—curing dreadful diseases, growing food where none could possibly have grown before, gestating human life outside of the womb, to name just three— some of the very people who enabled these discoveries are having second thoughts about where science and technology may take us. Some worry about their extraordinary technology tools getting into the hands of cyberterrorists. When the U.S. Government

———— ❧ ————

reconstructed the 1918 flu virus and published the genomic code on the Internet, two scientists, Bill Joy, co-founder of Sun Microsystems, and Ray Kurzweil, inventor and futurist, compared the genome to a weapon of mass destruction. In an op-ed piece in *The New York Times* they wrote, "No responsible scientist would advocate publishing precise designs for an atomic bomb." Others are concerned about corrupting the good that technology can do. Nuclear power can be good; nuclear bombs, not so good. Many scientific discoveries have provoked heated reactions from the general public. **The top seven in modern history are:**

1. **NUCLEAR POWER**

2. **PSYCHOTROPIC DRUGS**
   (especially when given to young children)

3. **GENETICALLY MODIFIED FOODS**

4. **EMBRYONIC STEM CELL RESEARCH**

5. **ORGAN TRANSPLANTS: WHO GIVES, WHO GETS**

6. **CLONING**

7. **EMBRYONIC MANIPULATION** (designer babies)

Some view embryonic stem cell research, cloning, and "designer babies" as threats to so-called natural laws. Others see tinkering with human beings as an insult to God. How far will science and technology take us?

Known as the fastest man on no legs, Oscar Pistorius had both his legs amputated when he was eleven months old because of a congenital defect. But he loved to run on his prosthetic legs. When he was old enough to be fitted with state-of-the-art carbon fiber blades called

Cheetahs, he could outrun almost anyone. The International Association of Athletics Federations said his new legs gave him a technical advantage, so they banned him from able-bodied competition. In 2008 the Olympic Committee overturned the ruling, opening the door to bionic performance surgeries.

Juan Enriquez can see farther into the future than most of us. He runs a biotech company, was the founding director of the Harvard Business School Life Sciences Project, and wrote the global bestseller *As the Future Catches You: How Genomics & Other Forces Are Changing Your Life, Work, Health & Wealth.* He told me about a young Olympic hopeful who had injured her knee and had it repaired through an advanced process called tissue engineering. But there was a problem: The new knee was so good that it made that leg stronger and faster than its biological twin. Her dilemma was whether or not she should replace the other knee, a perfectly good joint with no injuries, to make her more competitive. If biomedicine becomes the new steroids, professional ballplayers may have to be tested for mechanical body parts: "He's got that new bionic eye that lets him see the ball with 20–10 vision."

Stick It

According to contactmusic.com, Nicolas Cage is on the needle. He told them, "I feel that whenever I've gone through a major change in my life I somehow wind up getting a tattoo. It only happens once every seven years and I think it helps in some way." His back, arms, and who knows what else all sport elaborate images of dragons and symbols.

A few years ago I suffered a rotator cuff injury playing softball and went to see Dr. David Altchek at the Hospital for Special Surgery in New York. This is a hospital where people are rarely sick, but they are disabled or in pain. Patients often come in with twisted, broken, or shattered bones or joints and leave ready to play nine holes of golf. Unlike other hospitals, few people die there, so the place is very upbeat. Like other doctors at HSS, David Altchek specializes in sports medicine and is the medical director for the NY Mets. He asked me to raise my arm and when I winced at the point he had clearly anticipated, he asked the following question: "What level of performance are you seeking?" The implication was that he could not only fix my problem, but turn me into a competitive athlete. I quickly dismissed the fleeting fantasy of going pro and opted for physical therapy, which was good enough.

Hugh Herr, a double amputee, directs the Biomechatronics group at the MIT Media Lab. His goal is to merge humans and machines with special devices that mimic the body's musculoskeletal design and muscular and biological behaviors. Like others in his field, he's building a better mousetrap—better, in some cases, than the real thing. Herr told *The Los Angeles Times* magazine that if there are no constraints placed on what technology can be used, at some point the amputee athlete will have an advantage. That advantage is growing at warp speed because of the wars in Iraq and Afghanistan and the loss of limbs due to crude but effective incendiary devices. As a result, the U.S. Defense Advanced Research Projects Agency (DARPA) has poured millions into the development of brain-controlled prosthetics. And it's working. The DARPA arm is built to function like a biological arm in every way, replicating the human arm's 70,000 nerve fibers. The ability to program a complex neural network brings us one step closer to uniting the essence of man—our consciousness—with machines. Of course physical intervention is one thing. We accept plastic surgery, applaud organ transplants, and now think of artificial insemination as routine. What's on the horizon, though, is the stuff of science fiction writ large.

The Singularity Institute for Artificial Intelligence advocates the technological creation of smarter-than-human intelligence. They reference a number of technological pathways, including artificial intelligence (AI), that can achieve their goal, bypassing the slow evolutionary pace of Darwin in favor of what they call "convergent evolution." These "meta-Darwinists" believe that the merger of the computer and the human brain is inevitable and that our brains should be able to mimic the increasing computer power of modern technology. They say, "The entire five-million-year evolution of modern humans from primates involved a threefold increase in brain capacity and a six-fold increase in prefrontal cortex.... An

A Dog's Life

Dogs grow older seven times faster than humans. Scientists refer to this ratio as "parametric survival models."

artificial intelligence would be different." The singularitarians believe that because of Moore's law, AI minds will be twice or four times as fast as human ones. Joel Garreau talks about trans-humanism in his book *Radical Evolution*, and he outlines three possible scenarios: Heaven, in which our consciousness is portable and able to be placed into new physical models, allowing us to live forever. The second is the hell scenario, a super-smart Frankenstein that reduces ordinary humans to nothingness. The third is a virtual world in which technology competes with technology, solving problems as they are presented. No mention of war games, of course. Perhaps the most important quality of trans-humans is that they will be able to breed.

The Seven Bridges of Königsberg

If you've ever been in a maze and couldn't get out in one graceful turn, you probably felt like Leonhard Euler, the eighteenth-century mathematician who solved an interesting problem. He lived in Königsberg, where a river circled the center island of the city, then broke into two branches, around another land mass. Seven bridges were built to allow people to move freely from one area to another. Euler wanted to know if one could traverse all seven bridges, returning to the starting point without backtracking. He couldn't. He determined that only an even number of bridges would allow that course. These illustrations show why:

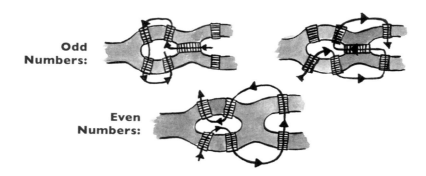

Odd Numbers:

Even Numbers:

CAN THERE BE LIFE
WITHOUT DEATH?

I first heard about singularity or trans-humanism from Ray
Kurzweil, who is preparing for his immortality. He takes 180
to 210 vitamin and mineral supplements a day, along with
weekly intravenous "longevity treatments," and maintains his
fitness and nutrition. He fully intends to live long enough to witness
and participate in the man-to-machine mind dump that he believes
will take place. The idea of a self-improving consciousness, like an
operating system upgrade, isn't a bad one. But it isn't human. That's
what concerns Bill Joy, one of the leading architects in computer
technology. "Why the Future Doesn't Need Us," his 11,000-word
essay in the April 2000 issue of *Wired* magazine, became a clarion
call to step back and think about the unintended consequences of
high-tech human tinkering. Joy offers two outcomes, and neither of
them resembles Heaven. The first is that we will cede more and more
complex decision making to higher-form robots because they will be
able to arrive at decisions faster and more accurately. We will
continue to do this until we become so dependent upon them that
they control us. Joy says that ending that dependency would be
tantamount to suicide.

The second outcome is even more devastating. We may control our
private machines, such as a car or personal computer, but the elite
trans-humans will control the large systems, giving them greater
control over the masses. Ordinary human work will no longer be
necessary, so the masses will be superfluous, a useless burden on the

system. The elite may simply decide to exterminate humanity, or, if they are kind, reduce the birth rate until the mass of humanity becomes extinct. They may care for humans like we care for endangered species, providing food, clothing, and shelter. If a human demonstrates a need for more than these necessities, like power, she or he will be "treated" so that the desire is eliminated. "These engineered human beings may be happy in such a society, but they will most certainly not be free. They will have been reduced to the status of domestic animals," Joy says.

Stinky Seven

A California chemist took on the odorous task of finding out just what is in the obnoxious liquid that a skunk squirts from its hindquarters as a defense against predators. This research uncovered three new components and a previously unknown chemical. That chemical, skunk musk, consists of seven major components.

WHAT WOULD DARWIN DO?

Charles Darwin shocked the world when he published *The Origin of Species* in 1859. To some, the idea of natural selection and survival of the fittest was heresy, opposing the Creation as described in Genesis: "In the beginning, God created the heavens and the earth." The Creation takes six days, followed by a seventh day of rest, presaging the seven-day week. **In these seven days there are seven divine commands spoken:**

❶ "Let there be light."

❷ "Let there be an expanse in the midst of the waters, and let it separate the waters from the waters."

❸ "Let the waters under the heavens be gathered together into one place, and let the dry land appear."

❹ "Let the earth sprout vegetation: plants yielding seed, and fruit trees on the earth bearing fruit after their kind with seed in them."

❺ "Let there be lights in the firmament of the heaven to divide the day from the night; and let them be for signs, and for seasons, and for days, and years."

❻ "Let the waters swarm with swarms of living creatures, and let birds fly above the earth across the expanse of the heavens."

❼ "Let the earth bring forth living creatures after their kind: cattle and creeping things and beasts of the earth after their kind."

Like other scientific discoveries, Darwin's findings challenged the status quo. In *The Origin of Species*, he wrote, "It is a truly wonderful fact—the wonder of which we are apt to overlook from familiarity—that all animals and all plants throughout all time and space should be related to each other in groups subordinate to groups, in the manner which we everywhere behold.... If species had been independently created, no explanation would have been possible of this kind of classification; but it is explained through inheritance and the complex action of natural selection, entailing extinction and divergence of character.... On the hypothesis of separate acts of creation the whole case remains unintelligible."

In a tip of his hat to the religious community, Darwin gave them a rational way out: "I see no good reason why the views given in

---

Seven Unsolved Medical Mysteries

❶ WATER ALLERGY This may sound impossible, considering that our bodies are around 60 percent water, but some rare individuals are allergic to water. They can still drink the stuff, of course. It's washing that causes the problem. A few minutes in the bath or shower causes their skin to erupt in itchy red weals.

❷ CHIMERIC PEOPLE Imagine going for genetic tests along with your children, only to find that you can't possibly be their biological mother—despite the fact that you gave birth to them.

This isn't science fiction. In one case, the mother was a chimera (a mix of two individuals). She was the composite of two nonidentical twins that had fused in her mother's womb.

❸ FOREIGN ACCENT SYNDROME If you wake up talking with a strong Jamaican accent despite the fact that you've never even heard a Jamaican accent before, then the chances are you're suffering from foreign accent syndrome.

❹ MORGELLONS DISEASE The symptoms: fibers growing out of itchy lesions, accompanied by a biting, crawling sensation, as if the sufferer is being attacked by a parasite.

this volume should shock the religious feelings of anyone.... A celebrated author and divine has written to me that 'he has gradually learnt to see that it is just as noble a conception of the Deity to believe that He created a few original forms capable of self-development into other and needful forms, as to believe that He required a fresh act of creation to supply the voids caused by the action of His laws.'"

What Darwin could not anticipate was that his brilliant observations would be hijacked by groups that would use his thesis as justification for their own twisted agendas. Eugenics, the "self direction of human evolution," was a social philosophy that advocated breeding rights for the chosen few. It was supported by the Carnegie and Rockefeller Foundations, and by a worldwide

---

5 THE MADNESS OF KING GEORGE The British king George III suffered major bouts of mental derangement, for which he had to be restrained in a straitjacket or tied to a chair. Scientists thought they knew the cause of these ravings: a genetic defect called porphyria. But in 2005 researchers examining a sample of King George's hair made a surprise discovery: high concentrations of arsenic.

6 PUTRID FINGER A 1996 issue of the medical journal *The Lancet* carried a distressing case study. A twenty-nine-year-old man had pricked his finger on a chicken bone five years previously, leaving him with an infection that made him smell terrible. "The most disabling consequence of the infection was a putrid smell emanating from the affected arm, which could be detected across a large room, and when confined to a smaller examination room became almost intolerable," the paper states.

7 TREE MAN With hands and feet resembling branches, Dede, a man from West Java, Indonesia, appears to be half tree, half man. But what is the cause of this deformation? Thankfully for Dede, this mystery may recently have been solved. The culprit appears to be a rare immune deficiency, which allows the human papilloma virus, better known as the cause of warts, to rampage out of control.
—*From* New Scientist *magazine, December 16, 2008*

A-list: H. G. Wells, Woodrow Wilson, Theodore Roosevelt, Émile Zola, George Bernard Shaw, John Maynard Keynes, William Keith Kellogg, Margaret Sanger, and Winston Churchill, to name just a few. Its greatest supporter was Adolf Hitler, who incorporated eugenics principles into *Mein Kampf*. Certain ethnic groups (Jews, for instance), along with the poor, the disabled, and homosexuals, were marked for either sterilization or extermination.

D arwin has been accused of fostering and approving of human selective breeding, often by people who want to denounce evolution in favor of intelligent design or creationism. They carefully choose partial passages from his books in order to paint him as a cold elitist who wanted to play God. But Darwin was clear about distinguishing between selective breeding among animals and humans. In *The Descent of Man* he wrote, "But excepting in the case of man himself, hardly any one is so ignorant as to allow his worst animals to breed. . . . The surgeon may harden himself whilst performing an operation, for he knows that he is acting for the good of his patient; but if we were intentionally to neglect the weak and helpless, it could only be for a contingent benefit, with an overwhelming present evil."

The many forms of life on earth are difficult to define, especially for scientists. But there is consensus that **life is characteristic of organisms that exhibit seven special behaviors**. Could these seven phenomena apply to the singularity?

➊ **HOMEOSTASIS:** Regulation of the internal environment to maintain a constant state; for example, electrolyte concentration or sweating to reduce temperature.

❷ **ORGANIZATION:** Being structurally composed of one or more cells, which are the basic units of life.

❸ **METABOLISM:** Consumption of energy by converting chemicals and energy into cellular components (*anabolism*) and decomposing organic matter (*catabolism*). Living things require energy to maintain internal organization (*homeostasis*) and to produce the other phenomena associated with life.

❹ **GROWTH:** Maintenance of a higher rate of synthesis than catabolism. A growing organism increases in size in all of its parts, rather than simply accumulating matter. The particular species begins to multiply and expand as the evolution continues to flourish.

❺ **ADAPTATION:** The ability to change over a period of time in response to the environment. This ability is fundamental to the process of evolution and is determined by the organism's heredity as well as the composition of metabolized substances, and external factors present.

❻ **RESPONSE TO STIMULI:** A response can take many forms, from the contraction of a unicellular organism to external chemicals, to complex reactions involving all the senses of higher animals. A response is often expressed by motion, for example, the leaves of a plant turning toward the sun (*phototropism*) and *chemotaxis*.

❼ **REPRODUCTION:** The ability to produce new organisms. Reproduction can be the division of one cell to form two new cells. Usually the term is applied to the production of a new individual (either asexually, from a single parent organism, or sexually, from at least two differing parent organisms), although strictly speaking it also describes the production of new cells in the process of growth.

F rans Lanting and his wife, Christine Eckstrom, have seen life on earth as few people have. Frans, an author of many books and a photographer for *National Geographic*, has spent more than two decades documenting wildlife in some of the most remote parts of the world. He and Christine photographed and recorded a tribe of chimpanzees in Senegal making spears out of tree branches, which the chimps used to kill and eat bush babies nesting in the hollows of trees. From simple invertebrates in the Galapagos to majestic mammals on the plains of the Serengeti, Frans has seen the beauty, the violence, the

Seven Years to Life

Frans Lanting is one of the world's greatest nature photographers. His award-winning books, as well as his publications in National Geographic *and many other magazines, celebrate the extraordinary diversity of life on earth and bring attention to all that threatens its existence. Lanting and his wife, Christine Eckstrom, spent seven years creating* LIFE: A Journey Through Time. *The project is an interpretation of the history of life on earth from the Big Bang to the present.*

Seven years ago I stood at the tide line of an estuary and began a personal journey through time. I wanted to visualize the story of life—the hardest thing I ever attempted. My aim was to create a sequence of images that could be seen as steppingstones of life on earth—from its earliest beginnings to the present. Chris and I went down to a remote lagoon in Australia hoping to see the earth the way it was 3 billion years ago, back before the sky turned blue. The stromatolites that exist there are living mounds of cyanobacteria, the first life-forms to create energy through photosynthesis. They release oxygen as a by-product, and the oxygen exhaled by stromatolites for 2 billion years is what we all breathe today. Stromatolites are among the heroes in our story.

It took seven years to bring this project to completion after the original experience I had standing at the edge of Delaware Bay, where I saw horseshoe crabs come out of the water in a timeless ritual of renewal. After Taschen decided to publish the book, we showed the work-in-progress to Marin Alsop, the famous conductor and brilliance, and the bumbling of earth's creatures. He doesn't want to tinker with them. He doesn't want to change the way they interact with one another. He doesn't want to tame them or make them cuter or more intelligent. He just wants to preserve them and the habitats in which they live. And he has good reason to do so because he knows how life begins. That beginning was 7 million years ago, when the first hominid, a distant evolutionary relative of *Homo sapiens*, was walking the earth. That ancestor is shared by humans and apes, and then the two species separated and followed their individual destinies.

director of the Cabrillo Festival of Contemporary Music in Santa Cruz, California, where we live. She connected us with composer Philip Glass, who loved the project. So with Marin, Philip, and other creative partners, we developed LIFE into a multimedia orchestral performance, with my images projected dynamically on a fifty-foot-wide screen while a symphony orchestra performs Philip Glass's music.

The final work, a one-hour symphony in seven movements, mirrors the organization of our book, *LIFE: A Journey Through Time*, which has seven chapters. In the back of our minds was the notion of Genesis and the seven days of the biblical Creation. The LIFE Project uses the principles of storytelling, which is part of what makes Genesis such an enduring narrative. We wanted to tell the story with lyricism and wonder without compromising the hard science. So LIFE is grounded in the theories of life science, with every fact vetted by scientists, but it's a story. It's a Genesis story for our time.

Science can help provide answers to many of life's questions, but its discoveries are often too complex and intimidating for many people to connect with their everyday understanding of the world. With powerful images and a compelling narrative, Chris and I tried to create a holistic vision of life, to reach people emotionally. Our mission is to inspire a sense of respect and wonder for our living planet, and to promote conservation at levels ranging from global initiatives to local solutions. LIFE is all about wonder.

THE CYCLE OF LIFE

G ive me the child until he is seven and I'll show you the man." This Jesuit maxim would have pleased Shakespeare, who catalogued the stages of a man's life in his play *As You Like It*. Although he didn't know it at the time, Shakespeare accounted for the life cycle, since the average age of a man of wealth in Elizabethan times was about forty-nine years. Other literary figures have also alluded to the seven-year cycles of life. Edgar Allan Poe's short story "The Masque of the Red Death" tells the story of Prince Prospero's attempt to hide from a deadly plague. He invites other nobles to a masquerade ball, which is to take place in the abbey of his castle where there are seven rooms, each painted a different color. Scholars speculate that Prospero is reliving his life, room by room, and that the colors—blue, purple, green, orange, white, and violet—represent his own life stages. The seventh room is "shrouded in black velvet tapestries hung all over the ceiling and down the walls," foretelling his demise. Of course another interpretation is that the rooms symbolize his seven deadly sins and therefore he must die this hideous death.

No writer or artist has exploited the seven-year-life-cycle theme more than Michael Apted, the British director, producer, writer, and actor who is best known for his documentary *The Up Series*. It began in 1963 when he was hired as a researcher on the first film, called *Seven Up!* Apted became the director of the series after that. The original idea was to show how social class determines success in life. They followed the lives of fourteen British children in seven-year segments: *7 Plus Seven, 21 Up, 28 Up, 35 Up, 42 Up*, and *49 Up* have told the stories of remarkable people whose lives in some cases were defined by the film. Although Apted says, rightfully, that the works are not scientific, they have enormous value as sociological studies simply because of their time line. Does life change every seven years? For some, there's no question about it!

Head Robot Team

The Takanishi Laboratory at Waseda University in Tokyo is a breeding factory— not for babies or puppies, but for robots. Based on the seven facial expressions identified by Dr. Paul Ekman, these robots can mimic the seven human emotions.

Happiness

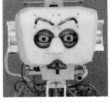
Anger

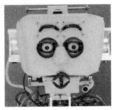
Surprise

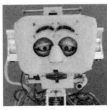
Sadness

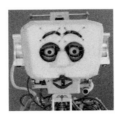
Fear

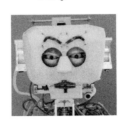
Disgust

Neutral

Living to the Seventh Power

For the just-turned-twenty-eight actress, life has always come in seven-year installments.

Christina Ricci is a fervent believer in seven-year cycles. "My mom told me, 'Every seven years, everything changes: your physical being, your emotional being, the way other people look at you. Everything'...Oh, God," she moans, mocking herself. "This is the kind of shit—if I go into the bookstore and ask for the astrology section, they're always like, 'Oh, aka the crazy-lady section?' That's where you'll find me. Yep, the crazy-lady section."

The thing is, if you look back at Ricci's life, her loony theory holds up: She's not so much a star as a Hollywood comet locked into a semi-leisurely orbit. And when she turned twenty-eight she saw "the end of a seven-year cycle and the beginning of a new one.

"It all comes back around," says Ricci, who swears that in her newest cycle she's not going to hide behind her notorious sarcasm. "I come from one of these hideous backgrounds where being sincere is like—ugh, you might as well kill yourself," she says. "It's fun to be sarcastic, but now I'm able to express myself in a way that's much more sincere. For whatever reason, I'm ready to refocus, and I've got my drive back. It's a new seven-year cycle. But then again, my mother told me a lot of crazy things."

The First Seven

Perhaps it's natural that Ricci, who grew up in Montclair, New Jersey, would become nineties cinema's beautiful young freak: Her mother is a former Ford model, *Seventeen* cover girl, and "starving socialite," as Ricci has joked. Her father is a therapist who specialized in "primal-scream therapy," which Ricci would overhear and playfully imitate.

The Second Seven

Ricci's acting career was launched via a spectacular grade-school freak-out. When her elementary school held auditions for *The Twelve Days of Christmas*, Ricci was in danger of losing the lead to another kid. So she hatched a plot only slightly more diabolical than the one she would later act out in *The Opposite of Sex*. Ricci taunted her rival so much that he socked her. When she tattled, he lost the part. "I've always been a really ambitious person," she says. "I guess that's the first time it really reared its ugly head. Apparently, my seven-year-old self was like, *You. Need. This.*"

A local theater critic noticed Ricci, and soon she was doing ads. She made her film debut in Cher's *Mermaids* at age nine and spurred a controversy over the sexualization of children when a pinup-style photo of a bikini-clad eleven-year-old Ricci ran in *Premiere* shortly after her cute-creepy turn as Wednesday Addams in *The Addams Family*.

The Third Seven

"From like fourteen to twenty-one, I got a lot of parts in paying films and became more of an adult actress," says Ricci, who also wrestled with more adult problems after her parents split up in 1993. She began the cycle as another slightly spooky sweetheart in *Casper*, but later she became anorexic and began cutting herself. And her roles started to mirror the intensity of her life: scandal-courting turns in *Bastard Out of Carolina*, *The Ice Storm*, *Buffalo '66*, and *The Opposite of Sex*, almost always as a strangely seductive outcast. "I think I've always been interested in playing people who are judged very harshly," she says. "I think that's why I get those parts when I audition for them. I hate when people are judged and misunderstood."

The Fourth Seven

Prozac Nation was a disaster, denied a domestic release by Miramax. With it, Ricci's career suddenly fizzled, too. "When I was twenty-one, I stopped being as productive," she merrily admits. "I kind-of-sort-of gave myself a break from any ambition that I ever had." Ricci racked up a few solid supporting roles, but almost everything else flopped. Her self-deprecating gloss on this cycle is that it allowed her to achieve relative normality. "I needed time to grow into who I am now. I needed some personal time." She laughs, realizing how ridiculous that sounds. "So, yeah, I took seven years of personal days."

The Fifth Seven

In this current seven-year cycle, Ricci says, "I'm totally down for more action movies, but I think I'd really like to find my place in sort of the higher echelon of dramatic actresses. Oh! And I'd like to play a spy."

A spy?

"Well, I'm so small," she says, cheekily mocking her oft-scrutinized frame. "So I always figured I would be the one they send through the air vent if something happened. You know: 'Can fit in small places.'"

—*Logan Hill. Excerpted from "The Tao of Christina Ricci"*
with permission by New York *magazine*

The biological seven-year life cycle has never been proven scientifically, although some have tried to measure cellular regeneration and have come close settling on the number seven. The problem is that different parts of the body have unique timetables—there's no magic moment when all our adaptive worn-out parts get replaced simultaneously. Simple creatures have an advantage over humans. A starfish, for example, can regrow one of its arms; humans are lucky if they can regrow the tip of the finger if they slice it off accidentally. But we can regenerate our livers from a mere 25 percent of its tissue. That's why live-donor transplants have worked so well. The mind, on the other hand, deals with seven-year cycles in a completely different way. At Time, Inc., one of the largest magazine publishers in the world, chief editors of their weekly magazines kept those jobs for six or seven years on average, followed by the proverbial kick upstairs to the ranks of corporate management. The theory was that after producing 350 editions of a magazine, the editor would burn out and want a new experience, a kind of editorial seven-year itch. And for the superstitious, there are seven years of bad luck if you break or crack a mirror.

A broken mirror aside, seven is a positive number in numerology and astrology. The founder of the website newprophecy.net has a theory called Base 7 Numerology. "It is a system of forecasting future events that is founded on the belief that the number 7 has special, mystical properties and may also be the paramount numerical factor by which time itself operates. The theory upon which the system operates is my own personal belief, following years of close observation, that history repeats itself in cycles of 7 years or multiples of 7 years. However, unlike true numerology, this is more a system based in mathematics, historical knowledge, and close observation of current events."

Seven plays a role in astrology, too. The seventh house was popularized in the musical *Hair*: "When the moon is in the seventh House and Jupiter aligns with Mars…" Somebody did their homework, because the seventh house represents intimate relationships and harmony, spouses and business partners.

Intimate relationships have been defined by the number seven for writer and author Sally Quinn. Her father, husband, and son have had the luck, love, and happiness that comes with seven.

Miles to Go Before I Beep

Even though Euler's seven bridges can't be traversed in one seamless journey, this one can: The Seven Mile Bridge in the Florida Keys connects the city of Marathon with Little Duck Key. The bridge has starred in four movies: *True Lies*, *2 Fast 2 Furious*, *License to Kill*, and *Up Close & Personal*.

Counting on Seven

Washington Post *journalist, author, and Washington, D.C., insider Sally Quinn founded and co-moderates "On Faith," a blog from the* Washington Post *and* Newsweek. *Quinn has written four books and is currently working on a fifth about religion in Washington. She is married to Ben Bradlee, the legendary editor of the* Washington Post, *and is the mother of Quinn Bradlee, a documentary filmmaker.*

I was an army brat, never living in one place longer than a year and a half. My father, William Wilson "Buffalo Bill" Quinn, became a war hero and ultimately rose to the rank of lieutenant general. During World War II he was chief intelligence officer of the Seventh Army in Europe and played a key role in the transition of the United States' intelligence service from the Office of Strategic Services to the Central Intelligence Agency. He later became commanding general of the Seventh Army in Germany.

Dad fought in the Korean War and commanded the Seventeenth Infantry regiment. Seven was always his lucky number. Maybe he passed that along to me, because seven has been my special number as well. I was born in July, the seventh month, a happy month. I have always had a thing about birthdays with a "7" in my age: 7 and 17, and 27, 37, etc. I would hit a low point before my birthday with a "7" in it; and then suddenly after I hit the magic "7," it would end up being an incredible year. Those years have always been happy years.

At seventeen I went to Mt. Vernon Seminary, a prep school in Washington, D.C. It was my fifth high school. The head of the school discouraged me from applying to Smith College, my first choice, because I did not have a consistent education. But I got in. It was another great seven because Smith was one of the "Seven Sister Schools," exclusive women's colleges that included Wellesley, Bryn Mawr, Barnard, Radcliffe, Mount Holyoke, and Vassar. (Today Vassar is co-ed and Radcliffe is part of Harvard University.)

At the start of my twenty-seventh year, I was out of a job and in despair, living at home with my parents. Then, during an interview for a job at the *Washington Post*, I met Ben Bradlee, the legendary editor. He recommended me to a fellow editor and shortly after that I was hired.

Ben and I were married when I was thirty-seven, and that same month I sold my bestselling book, *Regrets Only*. Several years later, in July, the seventh month, my son, Quinn, was conceived. He was born with many medical problems, including a hole in his heart. We were told he probably would not make it. But he was successfully operated on and he survived. He was severely learning disabled. When he was seven we were told by a psychiatrist that he would never have a life, that he would have to be immediately institutionalized, that he would never go to high school, never play sports, never have a job, never have a relationship.

I refused to accept that, and his seventh year was a turning point. I knew he would succeed. I kept him at the Lab School of Washington, a special school for L.D. children, and that year he started playing tennis and chess. Most dramatically, he began reading. Quinn won the art prize for the school that year, and he played the role of Tiny Tim in the Christmas pageant.

At age seventeen, Quinn went off to the Gow School, a special boarding school for dyslexic boys. His math teacher said he would never be able to do math. At the end of the year he won the math prize for the school, was a star tennis player on the school team, and won the award for the student who had most improved over the year. During that time I had taken a leave from the *Washington Post* and had written several books. I returned to the paper in July and proposed a religion website for the *Post* and *Newsweek*. "On Faith" has been one of the most successful features on the website.

The best part is this year I turned sixty-seven; Ben is eighty-seven and Quinn twenty-seven—a combination for true happiness. My website is going really well; Ben is in terrific shape, still working full time at the *Post*. He has his own website with Steve Pearlstein called On Leadership, and he's working on a new book. Quinn has published his first book, *A Different Life: Growing Up Learning Disabled and Other Adventures*, and he has his own website, a social networking site for young adults with learning disabilities called friendsofquinn.com. To top off my happiness, my son is madly in love with a beautiful girl who feels the same way about him. I can't wait to be seventy-seven!

Note: My mother was born in 1917 on January 27. My father was born in 1907. Quinn's new girlfriend, the love of his life, was born on December 17, 1976, at 7:57 A.M., weighing 7 pounds and 7 ounces.

Seven Big Life Changes for Kids

Dr. Michele Borba, a contributor to the *Today* show, says kids go through major life passages that need special attention and care:

1. First Day of School
2. First Failure
3. First Night Away from Home
4. First Move
5. First Loss of a Loved One
6. First Love
7. Graduation

THE COLOR SPECTRUM

*Isaac Newton divided the spectrum into seven named colors: red,
orange, yellow, green, blue, indigo, and violet (this order
being popularly memorized by schoolchildren using the mnemonic
ROY G. BIV. He chose seven colors out of a belief, derived
from the ancient Greek sophists, that there was a connection
between the colors, the musical notes, the known
objects in the solar system, and the days of the week.*

{ CHAPTER 7 }

Wonder

*I seem to have been like a boy playing on the seashore,
diverting myself now and then, finding a smoother
pebble or a prettier shell than ordinary, whilst the great ocean
of truth lay all undiscovered before me.* —Isaac Newton

I have never been able to figure out why people who are seeking a more rewarding and less stressful life want to smell the roses. As beautiful as they are, everyone knows what a rose smells like. Even if you live in a growing zone on the Arctic Circle, you can still smell the roses by buying Jo Malone's cologne or body lotion, or simply subscribing to *Vogue*, where you can sample the latest rose fragrance by sniffing perfume "scent strips." If you really want to commune with the natural world, gaze at the sky on a clear night. What you'll see with the naked eye can unlock some of life's mysteries.

It seems fitting to begin this chapter about the number seven with a discussion of its place in both science and religion, where constructs of belief and behavior sometimes collide with empirical knowledge and the pursuit of the unknown. Great societies have found ways to embrace both without placing a limit on love, learning, happiness, or friendship. Whether or not we experience seven-year life cycles, whether the "Magnificent Seven of European Astroparticle Physics" will be able to detect gravitational waves and dark matter, whether swimming in the Seven Sacred Pools in Maui can actually feel like one million kisses on

your skin, whether the seven common expressions of the human face will inspire future generations of personal robots, whether the seven continents and the seven seas will reconfigure as a result of global warming, whether the seven sister caves on Mars will ever prove that life exists there, whether there are seven heavens (or even one), our view of the world and ourselves is shaped by a combination of faith and facts and the knowledge that human beings can change that world. That seven plays a role in all aspects of our lives is testament to its power.

The number seven has a distinct place in the universe. Seven stars make up the Big Dipper, the brightest lights of the constellation Ursa Major (the Great Bear). Nearly all societies have named the configuration, which can look like many different objects, and each of these names may be characteristic of that culture. The British see the long-handled object as a "plough," which suggests the Protestant work ethic. In Germany and Eastern Europe, it's known as a Great Wagon, suggesting the harvest or, perhaps, Oktoberfest. The Finns call the image Otava, which means "salmon net." Like other Scandinavians, the Finns love to eat fish. Of course the French see the figure as a "casserole" or saucepan. Malaysia and North America are in sync—they see the image as a ladle or drinking cup (the Big Dipper). But the group winner would have to be the ancient Hindu astronomers, who called them Sapta Rishi, or the Seven Sages, representing great wisdom and power.

The Big Dipper is one of the first celestial groups young children can identify because these seven stars are visible to the naked eye. That's how Doug Zubenel found his calling. Zubenel, 51, became passionate about the night sky as a child and has been creating breathtaking photographs of the cosmos for the past twenty years. I discovered one of his stunning images of a crescent moon while digging around NASA's website. But the picture didn't tell the whole story: He had totaled his car just minutes before he took that picture. "The setting sun made it difficult to see the bridge until I was almost on top of it, and when I turned the steering wheel to avoid it, the car skidded and slammed into the bridge railing at fifty miles an hour." Doug wasn't hurt and his equipment wasn't damaged. "While I waited for the police and tow truck to arrive, I figured I might as well get the pictures I came to get."

The Moon Chaser

Like many baby boomers, I grew up with television. I was struck by the original *Outer Limits* series in the early 1960s, and resonated with Captain Kirk the very first time he declared, "Space, the final frontier," in September of 1966. There is always a defining moment, and mine came two years later. We were living in Woodland Hills, California, and I awakened on the morning of November 17 with an inexplicable compulsion to go outside. I stepped into our backyard wearing a robe over my pajamas, looked up at the sky, and saw a meteor. A few seconds later I saw another one, then another, and yet *another*, and asked myself, "What's going on?" I became filled with a joy I had never known. It was so intense that I actually grew nauseous.

I looked about the sky and spotted the Big Dipper. I had never seen it before. Seven stars, all of equal brightness, created a dipper-shaped outline I had only read about. I was hooked! Right then I made a decision to learn all I could about the night sky. I fully believe that when we make decisions in the throes of positive, passionate experiences, it can change the direction of our lives. A paradigm shift, if you will, occurs.

I received my first telescope a few months later, and as I looked at Jupiter for the first time, I had a vision of a large telescope, and a desire to share with others what I was seeing. In 2003, I completed that dream scope. A few years ago, I purchased a scanner and digital camera and hooked up with the Internet, which has opened a whole new world. I believe that what I have been given is a gift from God, and I am to share that for the enrichment of the lives of others.

There are other bright stars in the night sky. The Pleiades, a group of hundreds of stars in the Taurus cluster, has seven stars that shine so brightly they can be seen without a telescope even on a hazy night. They are known as the Seven Sisters, having acquired the name from Greek mythology. Alcyone, Maia, Electra, Merope, Taygete, Celaeno, and Sterope were all daughters of Atlas and the Oceanid Pleione. One myth tells how Zeus turned them into a

constellation in order to save them from that creep Orion, who pursued them for seven years. But wouldn't you know it, Orion becomes a star, too, and gets to be the first celestial stalker on record.

One odd and interesting connection to the Pleiades comes from the Japanese auto industry. Subaru is a Japanese word meaning "unite," or "gather together." According to the automaker, six Japanese companies merged in 1953 to form Fuji Heavy Industries, Ltd. The new corporation adopted the Subaru cluster of stars as the official logo for its line of automobiles.

Seven Role Models

During the Dark Ages, Europe needed heroes. And those heroes turned out to be saints. The Seven Champions of Christendom—Saint George, the Apostle Andrew, Saint Patrick, Saint Denis, Saint James Boanerges, Saint Anthony the Lesser, and Saint David—are patron saints of, respectively, England, Scotland, Ireland, France, Spain, Portugal, and Wales. They fought everything from dragons to rats to pagans.

Recently, another group of "Seven Sisters" has been located by NASA's *Mars Odyssey* spacecraft. These are entrances to what looks like seven caves discovered on the slopes of a Martian volcano. What's particularly intriguing to scientists is that the caves maintain a fairly constant temperature even though the planet warms up during the day and cools at night. Did life ever exist in these underground caves? Probably not the earthling variety, since the average temperature on Mars is a chilly −80 degrees Fahrenheit.

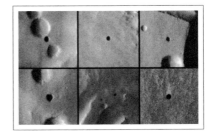

But life on Mars is a real possibility. Recent photographs of what appears to be ice under the surface confirms that the planet has water. If there ever was life on Mars, the ETs probably lived the high life, because the height of Mars' tallest volcano (89,000 feet) reduces Mount Everest (29,000 feet) to a foothill. According to NASA, "Mars might once have harbored life, and living things might exist there even today. Mars almost certainly has three ingredients that scientists believe are necessary for life: (1) chemical elements such as carbon, hydrogen, oxygen, and nitrogen that form the building blocks of living things, (2) a source of energy that living organisms can use, and (3) liquid water." If true, Steven Spielberg will probably be named the earth's first ambassador to Mars, a global title that would stand for peace, friendship, and free movie downloads.

It's not just chemical elements and growing conditions that sustain life. Without the atoms that bind those elements together, we would not exist. So says Sir Martin Rees, who may have the coolest title in the

United Kingdom: Astronomer Royal. If that doesn't do it for you, try this: In his book *Just Six Numbers*, which was written for laypeople like me, he identifies the numbers that define our entire universe and everything in it. Each of these numbers is a constant value that if altered or changed would mean the end to life as we know it.

For those of us who barely understand the physics of how a Slinky "walks" down stairs, the mathematical underpinnings for these numbers would be meaningless. So Rees doesn't complicate his thesis with mind-bending equations or explanations of string theory. Instead, he tells us how these numbers play a crucial role in our evolving universe. Of course the number that intrigued me is the number Rees says determines life itself. It's represented as ε (epsilon) = 0.007. "Epsilon defines how firmly atomic nuclei bind together and how all the atoms on Earth were made. The value of epsilon controls the power from the Sun and, more sensitively, how stars transmute hydrogen into all the atoms of the periodic table. Carbon and oxygen are common, and gold and uranium are rare, because of what happens in the stars. If epsilon were 0.006 or 0.008, we could not exist," Rees says.

Rees is not challenging Einstein's famous equation, $E = mc^2$ (E)nergy = (m)ass × (c^2) speed of light squared. But the two ideas are related because 0.007 allows nuclear fusion to take place, a much more efficient form of energy production than, say, a chemical explosion. He explains, "The nucleus of a helium atom weighs 99.3 percent as much as the two protons and two neutrons that go to make it. The remaining 0.7 percent is released mainly as heat. So the fuel that powers the Sun—the hydrogen gas in its core—converts 0.007 of its mass into energy when it fuses into helium." Simply put, 0.007 determines how long stars, and, of course, our own sun, live. It's also the number at the core of our energy and water crises since it accounts for solar power and hydrogen, a main ingredient in water.

Did Ian Fleming study astrophysics and create James Bond as an atomic character? Did he know that .007 is the core of our atomic existence? Fleming did rise to the rank of commander in the British Naval Intelligence of the Royal Navy and might have been exposed to some supersecret atomic "eyes only" data. Between 1941 and 1946, he did prepare geographic "reports" about countries with military operations. His research included the United States, which was hosting the Manhattan Project under the aegis of Robert Oppenheimer during those very same years. Jennet Conant's book *The Irregulars* describes how Roald Dahl and the British spy ring operated in wartime Washington. Fleming was recruited by the head of the Secret Intelligence Service for the Western Hemisphere, William Stephenson, a Canadian. "Fleming knew from his access to eyes-only documents that Stephenson, by carefully nurturing his unofficial relationship with the FBI, had already rendered 'innumerable services to the Royal Navy that could not have been asked for, let alone executed through normal channels.'" Fleming also takes credit for the original charter of the OSS as well as the plan for America's Secret Service.

Move Over, Superman

Ultra Seven is a popular fictional superhero and Japanese television series of the same name, similar to *Star Trek*.

For some, the best way to understand the universe is to experience it. Why else would anyone want to wrap themselves up in a hot, heavy moon suit, pee into an anatomically correct suction tube, and live in a tiny cabin in the middle of nowhere, surrounded by dark energy and black holes? The first seven astronauts to make the cut were assigned to Project Mercury, NASA's first

manned space program. The roster included Scott Carpenter; L. Gordon Cooper, Jr.; John H. Glenn, Jr.; Virgil I. "Gus" Grissom; Walter M. Schirra, Jr.; Alan B. Shepard, Jr.; and Donald K. "Deke" Slayton.

Dr. Laurence R. Young, Apollo Program Professor of Astronautics and Professor of Health Sciences and Technology at the Massachusetts Institute of Technology, knows a thing or two about space travel and what draws people to the outer limits. "We've always been bound by gravity. The entire evolution of biology on earth has been a 1-G experience. There's been a curiosity and drive to escape gravity. We love trampolines and diving boards. We want to emulate the birds and fly. We ask, 'What would it be like if I were not constantly forced down by gravity?' Artists have depicted at least 7 flying superheroes: Superman, Batman, Spider-Man, Iron Man, Wonder Woman, Captain America, and Captain Marvel. We've wanted to get around the inhibiting forces of gravity. Gymnasts do flips, hurling themselves in the air. Wouldn't it be wonderful to do flips in weightlessness? My own experience was limited to weightlessness in the parabolic airplane and this joyous, boyish, buoyant sense of freedom is like rolling down a grassy slope and giggling. Being in space is like escaping a boundary and a constraint."

Riding High on the STS-7

Lynn Sherr is an award-winning broadcast journalist and author, best known as a correspondent for ABC's 20/20. Her latest book, Outside the Box, *is a memoir.*

The first flight of an American woman into space was on NASA's seventh space shuttle, officially STS-7. On June 18, 1983, Sally Ride lifted off into a clear blue sky with the goodwill and crossed fingers of an exuberant nation. Her mission brought new meaning to the quarter-century-old manned space program. And new pride for America's feminists. Before the launch, she told me in an interview that her flight was "more evidence that women can do anything." I asked if she felt any special pressure as the nation's first female astronaut. "I do feel under some pressure not to mess up," she said candidly.

She did not. And when she worked the shuttle's robot arm, she showed just how versatile she—and it—were. As we watched from the Johnson Space Center outside Houston via a camera on a nearby satellite, Sally manipulated the mechanical limb so that it formed the number seven, presenting us the iconic image of *Challenger* orbiting the earth, wearing a giant "7" like an outsized charm.

Recently I asked Sally about the event, and she explained, "We actually figured out the arm angles on the ground before flight, and tried it out in the simulator. So we planned the '7' for the photos. No discussions about the magical nature of the number, just that it was our flight number and, hey, we could put the arm in that shape!"

Just lucky, I guess.

POWER PLAYERS

The number seven is synonymous with power and speed. The Boeing Company has used it to define their aircraft since 1957, starting with the 707. The commercial line of jets was originally going to launch with a simple 700 number, but the marketing folks thought it was catchier to add another seven. From then on, the 7-7 line was goldplated. Boeing's website claims that the FAQ "How did Boeing come up with the 7-7 name?" is the subject of a lot of conjecture. According to Michael Lombardi, "People who lean toward math and engineering are certain that 707 was chosen because it is the sine of the angle of wing sweep on a 707. It's not, since the wing sweep is 35 degrees and not 45. However, more people lean toward superstition and feel that the positive connotation of the number seven was the reason it was selected."

The 777, the latest in Boeing's suite of jets, can carry up to 368 passengers and is the largest twin jet in the world. The "Triple Seven," as it's called, has been around for over fifteen years, but they keep tweaking, stretching, or adapting the plane for different uses, including a freighter model that was introduced in 2005. On the drawing board is Boeing's 787, a fuel-efficient mid-sized high-tech luxury liner.

But high flying isn't the only thrust for the number seven. BMW replaced its "New Six" models back in 1977. And they never regretted it. The 7 Series has been a leader in luxury automobiles ever since and has made the company a fortune. They have been changing their line of cars every seven years since 1987.

When it comes to sheer power, speed, and drama, nothing beats NASA's Space Technology 7 (ST7), a New Millennium Program project that will study gravitational waves in space. Space waves are like ocean waves—they get more intense because of disturbances. Presumably an exploding star, otherwise known as a supernova, could cause such a disturbance.

How will ST7 measure these waves? It will carry a Disturbance Reduction System (of course!) laying the groundwork for mapping the curvature of space-time. Einstein would have loved this project, since this "scoliosis" of outer space is the core of his theory of general relativity. I'm not going to attempt to explain Einstein's theory. Suffice it to say that ST7 should accomplish its mission before Google decides to buy the gravitational wave spectrum.

I f you're on the fence about sky watching, author Timothy Ferris can close the deal. His one-hour documentary and his book *Seeing in the Dark: How Backyard Stargazers Are Probing Deep Space and Guarding Earth from Interplanetary Peril* are a veritable invitation to become a stargazer. Ferris, acclaimed as one of the best science writers of his generation, says astronomy is the most accessible and democratic of all the sciences. Anyone can participate by going outside on a dark night and just looking up. **Here are seven simple ways to become a sky watcher:**

1 To start, download Microsoft's World Wide Telescope, an extraordinary application that allows you to view the sky like a pro. You can research and view everything: the planets, stars, comets, and meteors, and learn about dark matter, black holes, and the like. (Google Sky, an enhancement of Google Earth, is an alternative, but it's not as rich or as robust as the World Wide Telescope.)

2 Once you've learned some of the most identifiable objects in the sky, try spotting them on a dark, clear night in a remote area with little or no ambient light interference.

3 Don't invest in a telescope right away. Telescopes zoom in on particular objects. Better to use seven- to ten-power binoculars, which afford a wider view.

4 Bookmark a few key websites that can deliver daily or weekly feeds on what to look for in the sky. A great one is Sky and Telescope (www.skyandtelescope.com). It's free, and the information and level of expertise are excellent. There are other informative websites that you should visit: The Astronomical League, the Rose Center for Earth and Space, and, of course, NASA.

❺ Keep a diary. Just like birdwatchers who record each species and where they spotted or heard them, you should record what you saw, when, and where, and what the conditions of the sky were. If you have the talent, add a sky graphic to your journal. Or take a digital photo of your earthly surroundings to mark the spot.

❻ Join a group or amateur club. You're not alone in the universe. There are wonderful clubs, outings, and people who share the same interests. You can join online through one of the websites mentioned or start your own group on Facebook.com.

❼ Check the night-sky calendar and plan an annual outing under the stars with your family, friends, or significant other. Pack a picnic, and feel the glory of the galaxy, even if it's right in your own backyard.

Energy Center

The seven chakras are the human wheels of energy that are at the core yoga mind/body philosophy.

THE SKY'S NO LIMIT

The seven bodies I'll describe anon:
Sol, gold is, Luna's silver, as we see,
Mars iron, and quicksilver's Mercury,
Saturn is lead, and Jupiter is tin,
And Venus copper, by my father's kin!
—*"The Canon's Yeoman's Tale"*
from Chaucer's Canterbury Tales

S ky watching, an ancient tradition, is how we came to name the seven days of the week. Depending on which language you speak and whether you prefer math or astronomy, the week is classified as either numerical or planetary. Either way, the number is seven. When ancients looked at the night sky they saw seven orbs: Mercury, Venus, Mars, Jupiter, Saturn, the Sun, and the Moon. Here's how the names played out in English, Old English, French, and by Planet:

English	Old English	French	Planet
Monday	Mōnandæg	Lundi	Moon
Tuesday	Tiwesdæg	Mardi	Mars
Wednesday	Wōdnesdæg	Mercredi	Mercury
Thursday	þunresdæg	Jeudi	Jupiter
Friday	Frigedæg	Vendredi	Venus
Saturday	Sæturnesdæg	Samedi	Saturn
Sunday	Sunnandæg	Dimanche	Sun

A seven-day week, or a twelve- or twenty-day week, was completely arbitrary. It was the "planets," with a little help from Genesis and the Creation, that nailed down the number to seven. But there were deviations. After overthrowing the monarchy during the French Revolution (1789–1799), the Jacobins wanted to overthrow Catholicism. So they decided that France needed a different calendar. With zero regard for countries in different climate zones, including their own colonies in the tropics, they named their months according to the four seasons: Winter was named for snow, rain, and wind; spring for planting, flowering, and growing; summer for heat, fruit, and early harvest; and autumn for harvest, mist, and cold. According to England's Open University, Britons scorned the revolutionary calendar. A satirical contemporary translation ran: Slippy, Nippy, Drippy; Freezy, Wheezy, Sneezy; Showery, Flowery, Bowery; Heaty, Wheaty, Sweety. Needless to say, the idea of one day of rest out of ten didn't go over too well with the French working class. The attempt to abandon the Church, its saints, and its holidays failed. The calendar was scrapped thirteen years after it was introduced in 1806.

O Brother, Where Art Thou?

Oedipus certainly knew how to cause trouble. He had two sons, Polynices and Eteocles. He decreed that, upon his retirement, the brothers would alternate ruling Thebes. But wouldn't you know it—Eteocles, the first to rule, dug in his heels and decided not to give up the throne. So Polynices got six other guys—Adrastus, Amphiaraüs, Hippomedon, Capaneus, Tydeus, and Parthenopaeus—to attack Eteocles and take back the throne. The warriors became known as the Seven against Thebes. In the end, as the myth goes, the brothers were killed and the only survivor was Adrastus.

CATHOLICISM AND CHRISTIANITY

The number seven has special meaning in Catholicism, and for that matter, in almost every religion you could name. Catholics and other Christians have the seven sacraments (Baptism, Eucharist, Reconciliation, Confirmation, Marriage, Holy Orders, and Anointing of the Sick), the seven virtues (chastity, temperance, charity, diligence, kindness, patience, humility [or faith, hope, fortitude, charity, justice, prudence, and temperance]), the seven joys and seven sorrows of the Virgin Mary. And what would life be without the seven deadly sins (lust, gluttony, greed, sloth, wrath, envy, and pride).* **Turns out that Mahatma Gandhi, the man who liberated India from British rule, created his own list of seven deadly sins.** They turn out to be far more thoughtful and thought provoking than the standard fare:

❶ WEALTH WITHOUT WORK

❷ PLEASURE WITHOUT CONSCIENCE

❸ SCIENCE WITHOUT HUMANITY

❹ KNOWLEDGE WITHOUT CHARACTER

❺ POLITICS WITHOUT PRINCIPLE

❻ COMMERCE WITHOUT MORALITY

❼ WORSHIP WITHOUT SACRIFICE

*The Vatican recently issued a new list of seven deadly sins: genetic modification, experimenting on humans, polluting the environment, causing social injustice, causing poverty, becoming obscenely wealthy, and taking drugs.

HINDUISM

Hindus view seven as they view life: with optimism, wonder, and joy. The seven Hindu earths or worlds accommodate mortals, celestial beings, the gods, radiant beings, deities, pure souls, truth. These worlds correspond with the seven worlds of consciousness: physical earth, breath earth, mental earth, intelligence earth, earth of latent divinities, radiant earth of spiritual fire, earth of supreme consciousness. **There are seven Hindu sages and seven marriage vows taken as the couple takes seven steps around a fire:**

1. To provide for and protect the household or family.

2. To build a healthy physical, mental, and spiritual life.

3. To earn and increase their wealth by righteous and proper means.

4. To acquire knowledge, happiness, and harmony by mutual love, respect, understanding, and faith.

5. To have children who will be healthy, righteous, and brave.

6. To have self-control and longevity.

7. To be true to each other and remain life-long companions.

Symbolic Sevens

The Complete Dictionary of Symbols claims that in Hindu tradition, the earth has seven faces, the sun seven rays. The sun symbolizes the power of God. In Islam, where the number seven symbolizes perfection, there are seven heavens, earths, seas, and hells.

CHRISTIANITY (CONTINUED)

Given the positive characteristics of the integer to Hindus, chances are they wouldn't appreciate the seven list from the Book of Revelation in the New Testament, the mother of all nightmares: the Seven Seals. These are the Antichrist, famine, plague, world wars, martyrdom, earthquakes, and, finally, total annihilation, courtesy of the seven so-called angels who inflict a series of hideous tortures on humanity. *Revelation* is an odd moniker for a narrative that results in Armageddon. Yet the Seven Seals has inspired great works of art and at least one madman in the name of David Koresh. In a conversation with FBI negotiator Byron Sage aired on the PBS show *Frontline* thirty-three days before Koresh and seventy-five other members of his religious cult, the Branch Davidians, were incinerated at their ranch during a government raid, Koresh argued that he alone knew the mystery of the Seven Seals. The following is an excerpt:

> **KORESH:** You do not know the seals, Mr. Byron. You do not understand the seals.
>
> **SAGE:** The only person, the only entity, that can open those seven seals is the Lamb of God.
>
> **KORESH:** Exactly.
>
> **SAGE:** Your challenge to us from day one to "just get somebody in here that can open these seven seals and I and all my people will come out."

KORESH: Exactly. These people remain here because I have thoroughly opened to them the seven seals.... See when it says in 22:12 "come the reward is me," it's very clearly identified that when Christ comes the identifying mark will be the knowledge of those seven seals.

SAGE: And so you are now claiming clearly and simply that you are the Christ.

T*he Seventh Seal,* an existential cinematic version directed by Ingmar Bergman, was released in 1957. In this interpretation, the fate of the knight returning from the Crusades hinges on a chess game. Considered Bergman's breakthrough masterpiece, *The Seventh Seal* won five major film awards and stunned audiences worldwide. In 1988, *The Seventh Sign* was released starring Demi Moore. It, too, was based on the Seven Seals and was thematically tied to the apocalypse, but it never received the critical acclaim of the Bergman film.

"Those are the seven deadly sins. You may choose any two of them."

JUDAISM

The real impact of the number seven in Judeo-Christian religion began with the Hebrew Bible, known to Christians as the Old Testament. It took God a mere six days with one day of rest to create the universe and all living species, according to Genesis. The Big Bang, evolution, and other scientific discoveries notwithstanding, the Creation gave the number seven a particular significance. E. W. Bullinger, a nineteenth-century radical British theologian who believed in extreme dispensationalism, dissected the Bible in order to find numerical patterns, repeated phrases, and other common elements. He recorded his findings in the work *Number in Scripture: Its Supernatural Design and Spiritual Significance* and wrote, "The number *seven* is stamped on 'the times and seasons' of Scripture, marking the *spiritual perfection* of the Divine Prophecies." The line between mysticism, religion, and numerology is fuzzy and fascinating.

In Judaism, seven means completeness as well as perfection. Seven translates into Hebrew as *shevah* or *shehbah*, from the root *savah*, to be full or satisfied. It's also pronounced *shiv'a*, the number of days of mourning (one "sits Shiva"). **Although the Torah is comprised of the five books of Moses, the number seven is an important marker:**

❶ God rested on the seventh day, the Sabbath.

❷ In Israel, there are seven days of Passover and Sukkot.

③ There's a seven-day purification ritual.

④ The jubilee year takes place 7 x 7 years.

⑤ From Passover to the Festival of Weeks, when the Jewish people were given the Torah, there is "seven times seven weeks," known as the Counting of the Omer.

⑥ Ever wonder why some companies offer employees sabbaticals after six or seven years? Chalk it up to Leviticus 25:3–4.

Six years thou shalt sow thy field, and six years thou shalt prune thy vineyard and gather in the fruit thereof; But in the seventh year shall be a Sabbath of rest unto the land, a Sabbath for the Lord: thou shalt neither sow thy field, nor prune thy vineyard.

⑦ Finally, and this is debatable, there are seven names of God in Judaism. Each name represents a characteristic of God's divine nature or of God's relationship to the Israelites: El (prominent), Elohim (powerful), Adonai (Lord), Ehyeh-Asher-Ehyeh (I am that I am), YHWH (Yahweh or Jehovah—Supreme Lord), Shaddai (God Almighty), Zebaot (Lord of Hosts).

Better to Light a Candle

If you've ever wondered why the traditional menorah has seven candles, you'd have to go back to the beginning. That would be Moses and the burning bush. The menorah is one of the oldest symbols of Judaism and was lit in the Temple of Jerusalem by olive oil.

ISLAM

Mehnaz Sahibzada, an Islamic scholar, acknowledges that seven is a perfect number among Middle Eastern cultures, standing for goodness and completeness. For Muslims, seven is even more sacred. In her essay "The Symbolism of the Number Seven in Islamic Culture and Rituals," she says, "The Miraj or Ascension story of the Prophet Muhammad (d. 632 C.E.), the Prophet of Islam, is of particular importance in reference to the miraculous nature of the number seven. According to Muslim tradition, the Prophet Muhammad ascended into the seven heavens during his lifetime in Jerusalem, either physically or spiritually, and came into direct contact with the divine. This story, also mentioned in the Qur'an, is a favorite among Muslims, and may be one of the reasons for the popularization of the number seven in Islamic societies." Other references:

- There are seven earths in Islamic tradition.

- Muslims walk between Al-Safa and Al-Marwah seven times during the ritual pilgrimage of Hajj.

- Seven circumambulations (Tawaf) are made around the Ka'ba in Mecca.

- There are seven doors to hell.

Dead Man Driving

In Gainesville, Florida, police issued seven tickets to a car parked illegally. They didn't seem to notice the dead guy in the backseat, possibly because of the tinted windows in his BMW.

The Seven Shared Beliefs

*The differences among Christians, Jews, and Muslims are profound. But the
similarities are just as meaningful. If we really want to find a road to peace,
we should focus on that half-full glass, and build on the possibility of finding
more interests and beliefs in common.*

❶ MONOTHEISM: Belief in one God. Christians believe in
the Holy Trinity (The Father, Son, and Holy Spirit), but the
three are one according to the New Testament.

❷ DIVINE REVELATION: Truths are revealed through
the word of God.

❸ DAILY PRAYER: Muslims must pray five times a day; Jews
are supposed to thank God every day for the gifts he
bestows; and Christians who follow Catholicism are to pray
seven times a day, while most simply say nightly prayers.

**❹ MUSLIMS, CHRISTIANS, AND JEWS ALL PARTICIPATE
IN RELIGIOUS FASTS.** Christians have Lent, a forty-day
period of denial leading up to the crucifixion and
resurrection of Jesus; Jews fast during Yom Kippur; and
Muslims fast during the month of Ramadan.

❺ PROPHETIC TRADITION: All three religions believe in
"messengers of God." Jews and Christians believe in Moses,
among others, in the Old Testament; Muslims acknowledge
many prophets of Allah cited in the Qur'an, the most
important being Muhammed. All three honor Abraham as a
great prophet. Abraham believed in the one and only God.
So if all three religions believe in Abraham, they would
logically believe in the same God.

❻ ALL THREE BELIEVE IN ALMSGIVING AND CHARITY.

❼ MECCA AND JERUSALEM ARE TWO HOLY SITES,
the latter shared by Christians and Jews.

HONOR, VIRTUE, AND EASTERN PHILOSOPHY

The country that has elevated the number seven to special status is Japan. For starters, there are the "seven lucky gods." These are deities from Japan, India, and China that represent luck, happiness, and good fortune. They are often depicted in netsuke carvings and look a bit like jolly gargoyles. These lucky gods, which stand for abundance, fortune, strength, culture, dignity, wisdom, happiness, and longevity, are synonymous with Japan's seven virtues.

"The way of the warrior," known as Bushido in Japan, is a code of ethics and behavior that was followed by all samurai warriors. There is no attribution given for the seven virtues, but they are primarily based on Confucian philosophy. If a soldier screwed up—was captured or blew a command on the battlefield—he was honor bound to kill himself. So he would take his samurai sword and gut himself. **These are the seven virtues, according to Taisen Deshimaru:**

❶ **GI:** The right decision, taken with equanimity, the right attitude, the truth. When we must die, we must die. Rectitude.

❷ **YU:** Bravery tinged with heroism.

❸ **JIN:** Universal love, benevolence toward mankind; compassion.

❹ **REI:** Right action—a most essential quality, courtesy.

❺ **MAKOTO:** Utter sincerity; truthfulness.

❻ **MELYO:** Honor and glory.

❼ **CHUGO:** Devotion, loyalty.

THE NATURAL WORLD

From the heavens to the earth we find the seven seas, the seven continents, and the seven summits, the highest among the latter being Mount Everest at 29,000 feet, and, of course, the Seven Wonders of the Ancient World, which included the Pyramids of Egypt, the Lighthouse of Alexandria, the Hanging Gardens of Babylon, the Temple of Artemis, the Statue of Zeus, the Mausoleum at Halicarnassus, the Colossus of Rhodes. World wonders have become a popular franchise. They come in a variety of sizes, shapes, and interests. But they almost always come in sevens. Many lists circulated during the Middle Ages. Here's a more recent list I like: Stonehenge, the Colosseum, the Taj Mahal, the Great Wall of China, the Porcelain Tower of Nanjing, Hagia Sophia, and the Leaning Tower of Pisa. But the latest list is like the *American Idol* of World Wonders because anyone can vote for the winners. The New Seven Wonders of Nature pays homage to our planet by honoring the environment. And the sponsors clearly love the number seven because the first round of voting will yield seventy-seven natural wonders. "Welcome to the second phase of the Official New Seven Wonders of Nature campaign! 261 qualified national and multinational nominees are participating to make it to the top 77. You have one voice, and you have seven choices." There will no doubt be some controversy, since there is already a list, which

---

Did Wyatt Earp Wear One?

The seven-pointed star, called a heptagram, is a traditional symbol for warding off evil and is the badge worn by most American sheriffs.

includes the Grand Canyon, the Great Barrier Reef, Mount Everest, the Northern Lights, Paricutin Volcano, Victoria Falls, and the Harbor at Rio de Janeiro. There are remarkable manmade wonders, too. One of the most extraordinary is the Millau Viaduct, part of the new E11 expressway connecting Paris and Barcelona. It's the highest bridge ever constructed at 1,125 feet. Just don't look down.

Native American Sevens

Seven is a sacred number to the Cherokee nation. It represents seven directions: north, south, east, west, above, below, middle (or center). Add to this the seven sacred ceremonies, which follow the growing season from March through November. But that's not all. The Cherokee have seven clans, each with a great name: Wild Potato, Long Hair, Deer, Bird, Blue Holly, Paint, and Wolf.

Any structure or area that makes the cut and becomes a "wonder" is an instant tourist attraction and is promoted in travel brochures and on sightseeing tours. And that means money. So, in the spirit of global commerce, here's a list you won't find in the guide books. **It's my "Seven Wacky Wonders of the World."**

❶ **WHERE ARE THE CUP HOLDERS?** Finally, an electric car you can believe in. It's ecologically friendly, smart looking, and flood proof. Huh? The car, called sQuba, can dive and drive up to thirty-three feet under water. Rinspeed, a Swiss company, built a car inspired by the James Bond movie *The Spy Who Loved Me*, engineered the sQuba to drive on land and then, by pushing a button, dive under the sea with the help of propellers and jet drives. Standard features include rechargeable lithium-ion batteries, rear-wheel drive for on-roading, and an oxygen supply—just in case.

❷ **WHILE MY GUITAR GENTLY CREEPS** Calling it the "biggest rideable guitar in the universe," Dieter "Didi" Senft thinks his giant guitar-shaped bike will win him another Guinness World Record. At more than forty-eight feet long and thirteen feet high, chances are no one will top it. Senft, who is known as El

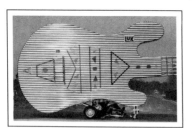

Diablo at the Tour de France because of his devil costume and devilish behavior, has built other wacky bikes, including a giant fish and a giant bike. But this one is more rock than roll—it weighs half a ton.

❸ LOOKOUTHOUSE The British press called this work of art by Monica Bonvicini "Loo with the View" when it was temporarily placed near the Tate Britain Museum in London. Its one-way glass allows the user of this fully functional toilet to see out, but no one can see in. So the existential question of the day is, Can privacy exist when you can see the hustle and bustle of the world—and even your former boyfriend—all around you? Only the Swiss can know for sure, since the permanent installation is in Basel, Switzerland.

❹ WHALE MAIL Even if you don't yet own a sQuba, you may be an underwater enthusiast, diver style. If so, why not send a postcard to your land-locked

friends from one of the five underwater post offices in the world? Some are staffed; others are simply mailboxes with scheduled pickup times (no deliveries that we know of). Try one at Hideaway Island in the South Pacific; off Japan's southeastern coast; at Malaysia's Reef Dive Resort; in St. Thomas, USVI; or at Paradise Island, Bahamas.

The Prophet

The seventh century could easily be called the Century of Islam. Around 610 A.D., the prophet Mohammed was in Mecca and had a vision of God. He began preaching a new religion: Islam. After his death in 632, the Arabian empire expanded to Europe and beyond.

❺ FOR COOLER CATS It's a piano. It's made of ice. And it works. It was created in China and unveiled at the 20th International Snow-Sculpture Art Expo in Harbin city in December 2007. The ice sculpture is a player piano with a repertoire of over thirty classical pieces. Tourists can also try their hands at "Chopsticks" or, if they're more talented, a Bach concerto. But they'll have to do it before the weather turns warm and melts the keys.

❻ BEND 'EM LIKE SONKIE Dutch architect Jan Sonkie decided to build his dream house. And that meant football, European style. The house is four stories high with at least one room on each floor. Talk about living in a fish ball!

❼ PAINT CHIPS OFF THE OLD BLOCK Ever since the pooper scooper laws went into effect, urban dwellers have not had to scope out the sidewalk for hazards or detours. Until now. Street artists who used to chalk it up to one-dimensional image have gone 3D. And the results are truly stunning. Like the work of Julian Beever, which can make you think twice before stepping on it.

The Seven Manifesto

S even is not just a number—it's a gift. It can lift your spirit and help you see the world in new ways. Seven has always been used to define time and space: the seven days of the week, the seven continents, the seven seas. And it's rather thrilling to think of so many brilliant scholars as proponents of its unique value, including a Greek philosopher, an Elizabethan playwright, and the father of cognitive science. But you don't have to be Shakespeare to benefit from seven today.

When used effectively, seven can put you in control of your life even as more and more electronic and digital intrusions are poised to undermine your happiness, your love relationships and friendships, and your success. I think of seven as my virtual Swiss Army knife. I try to use it to whittle away unnecessary meetings, e-mails, catalogs that overstuff my mailbox, and my own impulses to buy something I don't need. Try having conversations with seven co-workers instead of sending seven e-mails. You'll be amazed at how effective a face-to-face conversation can be. Or try to increase the number of times you physically touch your partner by a factor of seven. Or try this:

Your 24-Hour Day

- **7 HOURS OF SLEEP:** we know seven hours is necessary for good health

- **7 HOURS OF WORK:** this can be adjusted by taking an hour or two away from play, if necessary

- **7 HOURS OF PLAY:** this is time for family and friends and lots of laughs

- **3 HOURS FOR YOU:** daydream, take a walk, strum your guitar

Seven can become your manifesto, an elegant and personal way to "take back your life." I want to leave you with one more list. **These are the Seven Factors of Enlightenment from Buddhism, and they describe qualities that can be achieved by using seven:**

1. **MINDFULNESS** Paying attention to all around you; taking nothing for granted.

2. **INVESTIGATION** Learning about the world—education

3. **ENERGY** Being fit and ready to face the day

4. **JOY OR RAPTURE** Finding time for play

5. **RELAXATION AND TRANQUILITY** Allowing the mind to wander and rest

6. **CONCENTRATION** Achieving focus or flow

7. **EQUANIMITY** Being able to face the trials and tribulations of life with grace and fortitude

ONE FINAL FACT

The House of the Seven Gables in Salem, Massachusetts, is now a museum. It was built in 1668 for Captain John Turner and stayed in his family for three generations until it was sold to the Ingersolls, who were related to Nathaniel Hawthorne. Hawthorne's book, published in 1851, brought fame and attention to the house, and no wonder. The novel had it all: romance, mystery, intrigue, murder, and witchcraft. A movie was also produced in 1940. On March 29, 2007, the House of the Seven Gables Historic District was designated a National Historic Landmark.

{ ACKNOWLEDGMENTS }

This book would not have been written had it not been for Edward B. Burger. Ed and I met a few years ago at a conference in Charleston, South Carolina, where I heard him speak passionately, enthusiastically, and entertainingly about teaching mathematics to his students at Williams College. Our friendship grew over the years, and when I told him I was thinking of writing this book, he not only urged me to do it, he said he'd help. His encouragement and ideas were as valuable as the math items he wrote. I am grateful to him.

Believing in an idea—especially one that challenges traditional rules of publishing—is one thing. Convincing publishers of its value is another. Laura Yorke, my friend and representative with the Carol Mann Agency, had both the faith in the project and the expertise to guide the proposal. Her advice paid off and attracted one of the most respected editors in the business: Jonathan Karp. It takes one skill to know where to place the commas; it takes another to shape a book so seamlessly that the author thinks the changes were minor. They weren't. Jon's deft pen made the book work. And his collaborative style extended to the cover design of the book. His art director, Anne Twomey, and her designers created enough versions to fill the pages of another book about the number seven.

Designing the pages of this book was also a daunting challenge. The many elements, including the personal stories, the lists, the poems, the recipes, the photos, the illustrations, and the "marginalia" needed a real pro to weave them together into a clear, inviting format. That's why we tapped Douglas Turshen. Doug has been creative director of many top magazines, and we had worked together on *Child* and *Family Circle* while at the New York Times Company. Doug had always designed beautiful coffee table books, and I was thrilled when he agreed to design *Seven*.

The beautiful hand-drawn illustrations throughout this book are the work of Karen Leo, my daughter. She is a superb fine artist, but her passion is the avant-garde world of video and performance art. Take a look at Karen's introductory chapter drawings and see if you can find all the hidden number sevens.

When I told friends and associates I was writing this book, some came forward and offered their own special stories, puzzles, and anecdotes. My friend Joyce Ravid, the photographer, whose portfolio includes some of the most well-known authors of our time, offered to take my picture for the book jacket. What a wonderful and generous gift. Others took the time out of their extremely busy schedules to write or tell their own stories. **A very special thanks to the following people, who are listed in alphabetical order:**

WALTER ANDERSON: Chapter 5

LINDA AVILA: Chapter 3

DEREK BOK: Chapter 3

JERRY DELLA FEMINA: Chapter 5

SERHIY GRABARCHUK: Chapter 4

JEFF GREENFIELD: Chapter 5

FRANS LANTING: Chapter 6

DANNY MEYER: Chapter 1

JACQUELINE NOVOGRATZ: Chapter 4

KRISTIN VAN OGTROP: Chapter 3

MEHMET OZ: Chapter 2

SALLY QUINN: Chapter 6

GAIL SHEEHY: Chapter 3

LYNN SHERR: Chapter 7

WILL SHORTZ: Chapter 1

LIZ SMITH: Chapter 5

JERRY TARDE: Chapter 4

JOSH WAITZKIN: Chapter 2

DOUG ZUBENEL: Chapter 7

Shorter interviews were also provided by a variety of thoughtful and helpful people: Special thanks to Marie Brenner, Juan Enriquez, David Kirkpatrick, Dr. David Schretlen, Richard Wurman, and Dr. Laurence R. Young.

A book this complicated requires a lot of professional help. I'm so grateful to fact checker Blaire Briody, to photo researcher Gemma Ingalls, and to researcher Rachel Gutner. Each of these women made this book better by correcting errors, finding great photos, and digging into the world of seven to find that surprising factoid or anecdote that adds to the unexpected impact of the book.

Finally, writing this book in addition to maintaining a full work schedule has been a real burden on my husband, John. He's always been supportive of my projects, whether they've flown or fizzled. That kind of tolerance takes more than patience. It takes love…and sometimes a good baseball game or two to make up for the time we lost together. Thanks, John.

{ NOTES }

CHAPTER ONE SIMPLICITY

Eugenia Bone, "Feast of the Seven Fishes," *Saveur*, December 1998.

"Pick a Number from 1 to 10," macpolls.com, December 8, 2003, http://www.macpolls .com/?poll_id=332.

Lance Morrow, "The Shoes of Imelda Marcos," *Time*, March 31, 1986, http://www.time .com/time/magazine/article/0,9171,961002,00.html; World Notes Investigations, *Time*, February 23, 1987, http://www.time.com/time/magazine/article/0,9171,963620,00.html.

Miranda Hitti, "Hormone Leptin Tweaks Hungry Brain," WebMD, October 29, 2007, http://www.webmd.com/brain/news/20071029/hormone-leptin-tweaks-hungry-brain.

U.S. Census Bureau, "Median and Average Square Feet of Floor Area in New One-Family Houses Completed by Location," 2006, http://www.census.gov/const/C25Ann/ sftotalmedavgsqft.pdf.

Intel, "Moore's Law," http://www.intel.com/technology/mooreslaw/.

"Unless you've spent your adult life pursuing some sort of monastic ideal, chances are you've had days when you felt buried by your possessions. You know—the clothes spilling from the drawers, the toys busting out of the baskets, the dishes overwhelming the cabinets. Where does it all come from?" Elizabeth Fenner, "Had Enough of Too Much Stuff," *City Press*, August 23, 2008, http://www.news24.com/City_Press/Lifestyle/ 0,,186-1697_2381301,00.html.

John Maeda, *The Laws of Simplicity*, MIT Press, 2006.

U.S. Department of Health and Human Services, "Stress Hormone Impacts Memory, Learning in Diabetic Rodents," *National Institutes of Health News*, February 17, 2008, http://www.nih.gov/news/health/feb2008/nia-17.htm.

David Brooks, "The Great Forgetting," *The New York Times*, April 11, 2008, http://www .nytimes.com/2008/04/11/opinion/11brooks.html?_r=3&scp=1&sq=the+great+forgetting& st=nyt&oref=slogin.

Richard Saul Wurman, *Information Anxiety*, Doubleday, 1989.

William James, *The Principles of Psychology*, H. Holt and Company, 1890, vol. 1.

Mark Williams, "The State of the Global Telecosm," *MIT Technology Review*, May/June 2008, http://www.computerworld.com.au/article/191961/cisco_video_p2p_may_.

Alex Wright, *Glut*, Joseph Henry Press, 2007.

Michael Arrington, "Twitter Saves Man from Egyptian Justice," *Tech Crunch*, April 16, 2008, http://www.techcrunch.com/2008/04/16/twitter-saves-man-from -egyptian-justice/.

BIGresearch, "There's Never Been So Much Media-Multitasking!" Eleventh Simultaneous Media Survey (SIMM 11), July 1007, http://www.bigresearch.com/.

Edward M. Hallowell, *CrazyBusy*, Ballantine, 2006.

ABC News, "Life in the Slow Lane," broadcast May 9, 2008.

William James, *The Principles of Psychology*, H. Holt and Company, 1890, vol. 1, pp. 403–4.

David A. Bray, "Conceptualizing Information Systems and Cognitive Sustainability in 21st Century 'Attention' Economies," Piedmont Project, Emory University, April 2007, http://papers.ssrn.com/sol3/papers.cfm?abstract_id=991165.

Ibid.

Dan Ariely, *Predictably Irrational*, HarperCollins, 2008.

Terrt Durack, review of Spring, 28 rue de la Tour d'Auvergne, Paris, *The Independent*, July 15, 2007, http://www.independent.co.uk/life-style/food-and-drink/reviews/spring -28-rue-de-la-tour-dauvergne-paris-457089.html.

Hina's Tea, http://www.hinastea.com/Sacramento-Tea-Store.aspx.

Kathleen D. Vohs, "Making Choices Impairs Subsequent Self-Control," *Journal of Personality and Social Psychology* 94, no. 5 (2008): 883–98, http://www.apa.org/journals/ releases/psp945883.pdf.

Solarnavigator.net, "7UP," 1999, 2007, http://www.solarnavigator.net/solar_cola/7up .htm.

"Is This Your Lucky Number?" *The Independent*, December, 31, 2006, http://www .independent.co.uk/news/uk/this-britain/is-this-your-lucky-number-seventyseven -things-you-need-to-know-about-07-430258.html.

CHAPTER TWO HAPPINESS

Sylvilagus floridanus, Eastern Cottontail, Smithsonian National Museum of Natural History, http://www.mnh.si.edu/mna/image_info.cfm?species_id=371.

Positive Psychology Center, University of Pennsylvania, http://www.ppc.sas .upenn.edu/.

Mihaly Csikszentmihalyi, *Flow*, HarperCollins, 1990.

Tal Ben-Shahar, "Six Happiness Tips," 2007, http://talbenshahar.com/index .php?option=com_content&task=view&id=41&Itemid=56.

Associated Press, "Tiger Puts Away Mediate on 91st Hole to Win U.S. Open," *ESPN*, June 16, 2008, http://sports.espn.go.com/golf/usopen08/news/story?id=3446435; WorldGolf.com, "USOpen.com Sets Viewership Record During U.S. Open Playoff," June 19, 2008, http://www.worldgolf.com/newswire/browse/14319-USOpen-com -sets-viewership-record-during-U-S--Open-playoff.

Daniel Schorn, "Tiger Woods Up Close And Personal," and Ed Bradley, interview with Tiger Woods, *60 Minutes*, broadcast on March 26, 2006, http://www.cbsnews.com/ stories/2006/03/23/60minutes/main1433767.shtml.

David Brooks, "The Frozen Gaze," *The New York Times*, June 17, 2008, http://www .nytimes.com/2008/06/17/opinion/17brooks.html?_r=2.

"Thaipusam," based on a program by Siobhann Tighe for BBC World Service, updated January 13, 2006, http://www.bbc.co.uk/religion/religions/hinduism/holydays/thaipusam. shtml.

Josh Waitzkin, Biography web page, 2007, http://www.joshwaitzkin.com/bio.html.

Josh Waitzkin, *The Art of Learning*, Free Press, 2007.

Jonathan Haidt, *The Happiness Hypothesis*, Basic Books, 2005.

Jona Lendering, "Thales of Miletus," *Livius*, © 2005, revised March 31, 2006, http://www .livius.org/th/thales/thales.html.

Kathleen Freeman, *The Work and Life of Solon*, Ayer, 1976.

Zhang Guoqing and Ruut Veenhoven, "Ancient Chinese Philosophical Advice," *Journal of Happiness Studies* 9 (2008); 425–43.

Ronald Inglehart, Roberto Foa, Christopher Peterson, and Christian Welzel, "Development, Freedom, and Rising Happiness," Department of Political Science, University of Michigan, http://www.worldvaluessurvey.org/happinesstrends/.

Robert A. Emmons, *Thanks! How the New Science of Gratitude Can Make You Happier*, Houghton Mifflin Harcourt, 2007.

Jeff Larsen, of Texas Tech University, and Amie McKibban, of Wichita State University, *Psychological Science*, journal of the Association for Psychological Science (April 2008), http://www.psychologicalscience.org/media/releases/2008/larsen.cfm.

David Leonhardt, "Maybe Money Does Buy Happiness After All," *The New York Times*, April 16, 2008, http://www.nytimes.com/2008/04/16/business/16leonhardt .html.

Claudia Wallis, "The New Science of Happiness," *Time*, January 9, 2005, http://www
.time.com/time/magazine/article/0,9171,1015902-1,00.html.

Dang Le, "Notes from Buffett Meeting 2/15/2008," *Underground Value*, February 23,
2008, http://undergroundvalue.blogspot.com/2008/02/notes-from-buffett-meeting
-2152008_23.html.

Israel Vicars, "Warren Buffett on Simplicity and Happinesss," *Fast Company*, July 16,
2008, http://www.fastcompany.com/blog/israel-vicars/israel-vicars-cinemichigan
-bizdom-and-other-entrepreneurial-endevors/warren-buffe.

American Sociological Association, "Money Can Buy You Happiness but Only Relative
to Your Peer's Income," press release, August 14, 2005, http://www.asanet.org/cs/root/
topnav/press/money_can_buy_you_happiness.

"Happiness Can Give You 10 More Years," RTÉ News, August 14, 2008, http://www.rte
.ie/news/2008/0814/happiness.html.

American Lung Association, "Seven Steps to a Smoke-Free Life," http://www.lungusa
.org/site/c.dvLUK9O0E/b.33569/k.45E4/Seven_Steps_to_a_SmokeFree_Life.htm.

Ted Spiker, "7 Ways to Prevent Heart Disease," *Men's Health*, http://www.menshealth
.com/mhlists/prevent_heart_disease/index.php.

Roger Dobson, "Effects of Anger Last at Least a Week, Study Shows," *The Independent*,
November 11, 2007, http://www.independent.co.uk/life-style/health-and-wellbeing/
health-news/effects-of-anger-last-at-least-a-week-study-shows-399869.html.

Liz Hunt, "How Mystical Seven Gives a Nod to Big Ears," *The Independent*, December
20, 1996, http://www.independent.co.uk/news/how-mystical-seven-gives-a-nod-to-big
-ears-1315313.html.

C. Hublin, M. Partinen, M. Koskenvuo, and J. Kaprio, "Sleep and Mortality," *Sleep* 30, no.
10 (2007):1245–53, http://www.pubmedcentral.nih.gov/articlerender.fcgi?artid=2266277.

"Baby," World Book, World Book, Inc., 2001.

CHAPTER THREE LOVE

Eric Konigsberg, "Hundreds Honor a Life Known for Magazine Innovation," *The New
York Times*, September 23, 2008, http://www.nytimes.com/2008/09/23/nyregion/
23felker.html.

Gail Sheehy, "On Heartbreak & Resolve," *Tango*, Spring 2005, http://www.yourtango
.com/2006138/love-learn-gail-sheehy-2.html.

E-mail from Gail Sheehy, June 24, 2008.

Deirdre Carmody, "Clay Felker, Magazine Pioneer, Dies at 82," *The New York Times*, July 2, 2008, http://www.nytimes.com/2008/07/02/business/media/02felker.html.

George A. Miller, "The Magical Number Seven, Plus or Minus Two," *Psychological Review* 63 (1956):81–97.

Maggie Jackson, *Distracted*, Prometheus Books, 2008.

Alison George, "Love Special," *New Scientist*, 29 April 2006, http://www.newscientist .com/article/mg19025491.400-love-special-secrets-of-longterm-love.html.

John Gottman and Nan Silver, *The Seven Principles for Making Marriage Work*, Crown, 1999.

"Neiman Marcus Seven Layer Cake," AZ Cake Recipes.com, http://www.azcakerecipes .com/neiman_marcus_seven_layer_cake_recipe-2319.htm.

A. H. Cicca, M. Step, & L. Turkstra, "Show Me What You Mean," *ASHA Leader*, December 16, 2003, pp. 4–5, 34.

Willard Gaylin, *Talk Is Not Enough*, Little, Brown and Company, 2000.

Nina Brown, "Edward T. Hall: Proxemic Theory, 1966," Center for Spatially Integrated Social Science, http://www.csiss.org/classics/content/13.

Malcolm Gladwell, *Blink*, Little, Brown and Company, 2005.

Elizabeth Barrett Browning, "How Do I Love Thee?" Sonnet 43 in *Sonnets From the Portuguese*, 1845.

Alexander Moseley, "Philosophy of Love," *The Internet Encyclopedia of Philosophy*, 2006, http://www.iep.utm.edu/l/love.htm.

Linda Arking, "On Motherhood," *Child*, November–December1987. Excerpted with permission from the author.

William Wordsworth, "We Are Seven," http://www.bartleby.com/145/ww124.html.

Jeffrey Kluger, "The New Science of Siblings," *Time*, July 10, 2006.

Marie Brenner, *Apples and Oranges*, Farrar, Straus and Giroux, 2008.

E-mail from David Kirkpatrick, November 13, 2008.

"Aristotle's Ethics," *Stanford Encyclopedia of Philosophy*, [2001], revised 2007, http://plato .stanford.edu/entries/aristotle-ethics/.

Robert Dunbar, *Grooming, Gossip, and the Evolution of Language*, Harvard University Press, 1997.

"Thinking about Brain Size…," *Serendip*, last modified March 7, 2003, http://serendip .brynmawr.edu/bb/kinser/Int3.html.

Joseph Epstein, *Friendship*, Houghton Mifflin Harcourt, 2006.

Plutarch, "Moralia," Loeb Classical Library, 1928, vol. 2, pp. 45–69.

Carl Bode, *Collected Poems of Henry Thoreau*. Enlarged ed. Johns Hopkins University Press, 1965.

Marc Bekoff, "Do Animals Have Emotions?" *New Scientist*, May 23, 2007, http://www .newscientist.com/article/mg19426051.300-do-animals-have-emotions.html?page=1.

Andy Simmons, "A Visit to the Elephant Sanctuary," *Reader's Digest*, November 2007, http://www.rd.com/your-america-inspiring-people-and-stories/life-and-death-at-the -elephant-sanctuary/article50111.html.

"What Price Friendship? For Some Pet Owners, There's No Limit," *The New York Times*, July 23, 2007.

Joanna Sugden, "Students Ask to Take Pets to Lectures," *The Times Online*, September 11, 2008, http://www.timesonline.co.uk/tol/news/uk/education/article4733758.ece.

"How Close Are People and Pets?" *The Times Online*, March 8, 2008, http://women .timesonline.co.uk/tol/life_and_style/women/body_and_soul/article3503544.ece.

Michael Pakaluk, *Other Selves*, Hackett Publishing, 1991, p. 182.

Ruth Gledhill, "Why Do We Believe in God? £2m Study Prays for Answer," *The Times Online*, February 19, 2008, http://www.timesonline.co.uk/tol/comment/faith/ article3393198.ece; Associated Press, "Oxford to Study Faith in God," February 19, 2008, http://www.rawstory.com/news/mochila/Oxford_to_study_faith_in_God_ 02192008.html.

Ibid.

Summary of Edward J. Larson and Larry Witham, "Leading Scientists Still Reject God" (*Nature*, July 23, 1998), http://www.lhup.edu/~dsimanek/sci_relig.htm.

Richard Dawkins, "An Atheist's Call to Arms," talk filmed February 2002, Monterey, CA, *TED*, http://www.ted.com/index.php/talks/richard_dawkins_on_militant_atheism .html.

Deepak Chopra, "Debunking 'The God Delusion,'" *Beliefnet*, 2007, http://www.beliefnet .com/Holistic-Living/2007/02/Debunking-The-God-Delusion-Part-1.aspx.

"Belief-O-Matic," *Beliefnet*, 2000–2008, http://www.beliefnet.com/Entertainment/ Quizzes/BeliefOMatic.aspx.

Seinfeld, episode no. 23, written by Alec Berg and Jeff Schaffer, directed by Andy Ackerman, originally broadcast February 1, 1996, http://www.seinfeldscripts.com/ TheSeven.html.

Associated Press, "After 40 Years, Interracial Marriage Flourishing," April 15, 2007, http://www.msnbc.msn.com/id/18090277/.

David Smith, "Proof! Just Six Degrees of Separation Between Us," *The Observer*, August 3, 2008, http://www.guardian.co.uk/technology/2008/aug/03/internet.email.

Dr. Joyce Brothers, "7 Lies Men Tell Women," *Reader's Digest*, http://www.rd.com/ 7-lies-men-tell-women/article15355.html.

CHAPTER 4 LEARNING

Like humans, a giraffe only has seven neck bones. http://zooplace.com/giraffe.htm; http:// animals.howstuffworks.com/mammals/giraffe-info.htm/printable.

Oliver Sacks, *Musicophilia*, Knopf, 2007.

"Profile: Brain scientist Dr. Joe Z. Tsien on Learning and Memory," TS-Si News Service, March 30, 2008, http://www.ts-si.org/neuroscience/3081-profile-brain-scientist-dr-joe -z-tsien-on-learning-and-memory.html.

Kate Melville, "Instant Replay—Building Long-Term Memory," Scienceagogo.com, http:// www.scienceagogo.com/news/20001012032303data_trunc_sys.shtml.

Joe Burris, "A Beautiful Mind: Andrew Engel Didn't Let a Brain Tumor Stop Him," *Baltimore Sun*, May 23, 2007.

"Information Pollution," Jakob Nielsen's Alertbox, August 11, 2003, http://www.useit .com/alertbox/20030811.html.

Jakob Nielsen, "IM, Not IP (Information Pollution)," *ACM Queue*, January 28, 2004, http://queue.acm.org/detail.cfm?id=966731.

Andy Guess, "Hey, You! Pay Attention!" *Inside Higher Education*, April 18, 2008, http:// www.insidehighered.com/news/2008/04/18/laptops.

David A. Bray, "Information Pollution, Knowledge Overload, Limited Attention Spans, and Our Responsibilities as IS Professionals," Emory University, [February 15, 2007], last revised May 9, 2008, http://papers.ssrn.com/sol3/papers.cfm?abstract_id =962732.

Nicholas Carr, "Is Google Making Us Stupid?" *Atlantic*, July/August 2008, http://www .theatlantic.com/doc/by/nicholas_carr.

Michael Agger, "Lazy Eyes: How We Read Online," *Slate*, June 13, 2008, http://www.slate.com/id/2193552/.

Motoko Rich, "Literacy Debate: Online, R U Really Reading?" *The New York Times*, July 27, 2008, http://www.nytimes.com/2008/07/27/books/27reading.html?_r=1.

Mark Bauerlein, *The Dumbest Generation*, Penguin, 2008, quote on jacket.

Jesse White, Secretary of State, Illinois, "Distracted Drivers Task Force Final Report," http://www.cyberdriveillinois.com/departments/drivers/traffic_safety/ddtaskforcefinalreport08.pdf.

Jack Broom, "Have You Ever Made Coleslaw While Driving?" *The Seattle Times*, December 7, 2006.

"Engineer in Deadly LA Train Crash Was Texting," *The Washington Post*, September 18, 2008.

Christopher D. Wickens, Jason S. McCarley, Amy L. Alexander, Lisa C. Thomas, Michael Ambinder, and Sam Zheng, "Attention-Situation Awareness (A-SA) Model of Pilot Error," technical report prepared for NASA Ames Research Center, Moffett Field, CA, 2005, http://human-factors.arc.nasa.gov/ihi/hcsl/publications/Wickens_AHFD_04_15.pdf.

Dr. Gary Small, "Research Shows That Internet Is Rewiring Our Brains," *UCLA Today*, 2008, http://www.today.ucla.edu/portal/ut/PRN-081015_gary-small-ibrain.aspx.

Claudia Wallis, "What Makes Teens Tick," *Time*, September 26, 2008, http://www.time.com/time/magazine/article/0,9171,994126,00.html.

"Inside the Teenage Brain," *Frontline* special, PBS, broadcast January 31, 2002, http://www.pbs.org/wgbh/pages/frontline/shows/teenbrain/interviews/giedd.html.

Howard Gardner, "Intelligence in Seven Steps," New Horizons for Learning website, 1991, http://www.newhorizons.org/future/Creating_the_Future/crfut_gardner.html.

Daniel Goleman, *Emotional Intelligence*, Bantam, 1995.

Christina Bielaszka-DuVernay, "Hiring for Emotional Intelligence," *Harvard Management Update* 13, no. 11 (November 2008), http://harvardbusiness.org.

Nitza L. Morales, "Workplace Emotional Intelligence," Genos Pty Ltd.

Sarah Spinks, "Adolescents and Sleep," *Frontline*, PBS website, http://www.pbs.org/wgbh/pages/frontline/shows/teenbrain/from/sleep.html.

George Siemens, "Connectivism: A Learning Theory for the Digital Age," *elearnspace*, December 12, 2004.

David Brooks, "Lost in the Crowd," *The New York Times*, December 15, 2008, http://www.nytimes.com/2008/12/16/opinion/16brooks.html?_r=1.

Daniel Swingley, "Baby Talk," *Current Directions in Psychological Science*, October 2008.

Kerry E. Jordan and Elizabeth M. Brannon, "The Multisensory Representation of Number in Infancy, *Proceedings of the National Academy of Sciences of the United States of America*, January 7, 2006.

T. Berry Brazelton, M.D., *Touchpoints: Your Child's Emotional and Behavioral Development*, Da Capo Lifelong Books, 1992.

Bernie Trilling, *Toward Learning Societies and the Global Challenges for Learning-With-ICT*, Oracle Education Foundation, 2005, http://archive.techlearning.com/techlearning/pdf/events/techforum/ny05/Toward_Learning_Societies.pdf.

Gary Jones, Frank E. Ritter, and David J. Wood, "A Cognitive Architecture to Examine What Develops," *Psychological Science*, March 2000.

"'Rule of Seven' Makes Learning Lists Manageable," Parent Institute, 2008, http://www.schoolfamily.com/school-family-articles/article/6093-rule-of-seven-makes-learning-lists-manageable.

Websites about the documentary *Run Granny Run*, www.grannyd.com; http://www.myspace.com/rungrannyrun.

"The Seven Liberal Arts," *Catholic Encyclopedia*, www.newadvent.org/cathen/01760a.htm.

Plutarch, *De liberis educandis*, Loeb Classical Library, 1927, vol. 1.

"Wabash National Study of Liberal Arts Education," Center of Inquiry in the Liberal Arts at Wabash College, under the direction of Dr. Charles F. Blaich, and in collaboration with research teams from the University of Iowa, led by Dr. Ernest T. Pascarella; the University of Michigan, led by Dr. Patricia M. King; and Miami University (Ohio), led by Dr. Marcia Baxter Magolda. ACT, Inc., under the direction of Dr. Michael J. Valiga, 2006–.

A. W. Chickering and Z. F. Gamson, "Applying the Seven Principles for Good Practice in Undergraduate Education." *New Directions for Teaching and Learning* 47 (1991).

Michael Engle, "The 7 Steps of the Research Process," the Olin and Uris Libraries at Cornell University, revised October 30, 2008, http://www.library.cornell.edu/olinuris/ref/research/skill1.htm.

Naomi J. Halas, "Seven Steps to Success in Graduate School (and Beyond)," http://www.brynmawr.edu/sandt/2001_october/research.html.

Dewey Decimal Classification (DDC) Review Schedule, Online Computer Library Center, Inc., revised September 14, 2005, http://www.oclc.org/DEWEY/discussion/ papers/reviewschedule.htm.

Robert L. Park, "The Seven Warning Signs of Bogus Science," *Chronicle of Higher Education*, January 31, 2003, http://chronicle.com/free/v49/i21/21b02001.htm.

Gina Telaroli, "Sidney Lumet on the Benefits of High Def Video," *Take Part*, September 17, 2008, http://www.takepart.com/blog/2008/09/17/sidney-lumet-on -the-benefits-of-high-def-video/.

Judy Steed, "It's Never Too Late to Grow Your Brain," *Toronto Star*, November 13, 2008, http://www.thestar.com/Atkinson2008/article/535618.

Global Poker Strategic Thinking Society website, www.gpsts.org.

Serhiy Grabarchuk, "Seven Puzzles for G4G7," www.ageofpuzzles.com.

National Scrabble Association, "History of Scrabble," www.scrabble-assoc.com.

Poetic Techniques: OULIPO, Poets.org website, http://www.poets.org/viewmedia .php/prmMID/5785.

Tara Parker-Pope, "Seven-Word Wisdom: The Contest," *The New York Times*, January 17, 2008, http://well.blogs.nytimes.com/2008/01/17/seven-word-wisdom-the -contest/.

History of the World in Seven Minutes, video, World History for Us All, San Diego State University in cooperation with the National Center for History in the Schools at UCLA, http://worldhistoryforusall.sdsu.edu.

U.S. Department of the Interior, "Water Properties: pH, Water Science for Schools," November 7, 2008, http://ga.water.usgs.gov/edu/phdiagram.html.

Denis Campbell, "Simple Ways to Make Yourself Far Cleverer," *The Guardian*, March 5, 2006, http://www.guardian.co.uk/science/2006/mar/05/media.bbc.

Constitution of the United States of America, Seventh Amendment, http://www .gpoaccess.gov/constitution/html/amdt7.html.

"Is This Your Lucky Number?" *The Independent*, December 31, 2006, http://www .independent.co.uk/news/uk/this-britain/is-this-your-lucky-number-seventyseven -things-you-need-to-know-about-07-430258.html.

CHAPTER FIVE WINNING

"Seven-Spot Ladybird," *Science and Nature: Animals*, BBC, http://www.bbc.co.uk/nature/ wildfacts/factfiles/412.shtml.

Michael Kress, "All-Star Christian," interview with Mike Piazza, *Beliefnet*, 2007, http://www.beliefnet.com/Entertainment/Celebrities/All-Star-Christian.aspx.

W. Russ Payne, "Aristotle on Virtue," Bellevue Community College, http://facweb.bcc.ctc.edu/wpayne/aristotle_on_virtue.htm.

Aristotle, *Nicomachean Ethics*, trans. J. A. K. Tomson, Table of Virtues and Vices, posted on website by George Irbe, 2000, http://pages.interlog.com/~girbe/virtuesvices.html.

Stephen R. Covey, *The 7 Habits of Highly Effective People*, Free Press, 1989.

Aristotle quoted at http://www.wisdomquotes.com/002494.html.

"Aristotle on Causality," *Stanford Encyclopedia of Philosophy*, [January 11, 2006], revised April 22, 2008, http://plato.stanford.edu/entries/aristotle-causality/#FouCau.

James O'Toole, *Creating the Good Life*, Rodale, 2005.

Aristotle, *Nicomachean Ethics*, trans. W. D. Ross, available on the Internet Classics Archive by Daniel C. Stevenson, Web Atomics, 1994–2000, http://classics.mit.edu/Aristotle/nicomachaen.mb.txt.

Sandra Lynch, *Philosophy and Friendship*, Edinburgh University Press, 2005.

Aristotle, *Nicomachean Ethics*, trans. W. D. Ross, available on the Internet Classics Archive by Daniel C. Stevenson, Web Atomics, 1994–2000, http://classics.mit.edu/Aristotle/nicomachaen.mb.txt.

Alfred Edward Taylor, *Aristotle*, Courier Dover Publications, 1955, p. 107.

Aristotle quoted in *Classic Quotes*, http://www.quotationspage.com/quote/28890.html.

Max Wertheimer, "Gestalt Theory" ("Über Gestalttheorie," an address before the Kant Society, Berlin, December 7, 1924), trans. Willis D. Ellis in his *Source Book of Gestalt Psychology* by Willis D. Ellis, Harcourt, Brace and Company, 1938; reprinted by the Gestalt Journal Press, 1997, http://gestalttheory.net/archive/wert1.html.

R. Buckminster Fuller, in collaboration with E. J. Applewhite, *Synergetics*, Macmillan, 1975; available online at http://www.rwgrayprojects.com/synergetics/s01/p0100.html.

Ross Dawson, "Future of Media Report," Future Exploration Network, July 2008.

Howard Fineman, "The 'Obama Way': Seven Steps to Success," Nov. 4, 2008, http://www.msnbc.msn.com/id/27523773/.

Malcolm Gladwell, *Outliers*, Little, Brown and Company, 2008.

"Liz Smith," Information Please® Database, Pearson Education, Inc., 2007, http://www.infoplease.com/ipea/A0880198.html.

Craig Wilson, "Saturday's Date—07/07/07—Gives Birth to Fortune Frenzy," *USA Today*, July 5, 2007, http://www.usatoday.com/life/people/2007-07-04-seven_N.htm.

Is July 7, 2007, Your Lucky Day? Religion Expert Available to Discuss Biblical Significance of the Number 7, *Newswise*, University of New Hampshire, June 13, 2007, http://www.newswise.com/articles/view/530804/.

Alesia Matson, *7 Mysteries*, Metaphor Publications, 2004.

Mark Schumacher, "Shichifukujin: Seven Lucky Gods of Japan," www .onmarkproductions.com, March 28, 2007, http://www.onmarkproductions.com/ html/seven.shtml.

"Dice Probability Basics," *The Wizard of Odds*, http://wizardofodds.com/gambling/ dice.html.

Clifton Brown, "Golf; Shinnecock Shows Teeth, and Field Retreats," *The New York Times*, June 20, 2004, http://www.nytimes.com/2004/06/20/sports/golf-shinnecock -shows-teeth-and-field-retreats.html.

"In China, Think Things Over Seven Times before Making Your Move," *Universia -Knowledge@Wharton*, July 13, 2005, http://www.wharton.universia.net/index.cfm?fa =viewArticle&id=994&language=english&specialId=.

Www.usasevens.com; http://ur7s.com/tournaments/usasevens.

CHAPTER SIX LIFE

B. A. Robinson, "Coming of Age Rituals in Many Faiths and Countries," ReligiousTolerance.org, June 6, 2004, updated March 13, 2006, http://www .religioustolerance.org/wicpuber.htm.

"Confirmation," *BBC Religion and Ethics*, British Broadcasting Corporation, August 21, 2006, http://www.bbc.co.uk/religion/religions/christianity/ritesrituals/confirmation_ print.html.

Ray Kurzweil and Bill Joy, "Recipe for Destruction," *The New York Times*, Op-Ed, October 17, 2005.

Joshua Robinson and Alan Schwarz, "Olympic Dream Stays Alive, on Synthetic Legs," *The New York Times*, May 17, 2008, http://www.nytimes.com/2008/05/17/sports/ olympics/17runner.html?_r=1.

Juan Enriquez bio, Biotechonomy website, 2003, http://www.biotechonomy.com/ juan.htm.

Jeannine Stein, "Faster, Better, Stronger?" *The Los Angeles Times*, July 23, 2007.

Sarah Adee, "Dean Kamen's 'Luke Arm' Prosthesis Readies for Clinical Trials," *ieee Spectrum Online*, February 2008, http://www.spectrum.ieee.org/feb08/5957/2.

"Overview: What Is the Singularity?" Singularity Institute for Artificial Intelligence website, 2007, http://www.singinst.org/overview/whatisthesingularity.

Joel Garreau, *Radical Evolution*, Doubleday, 2005.

Gary Wolf, "Futurist Ray Kurzweil Pulls Out All the Stops (and Pills) to Live to Witness the Singularity," *Wired*, March 2008, http://www.wired.com/medtech/drugs/magazine/1604/ff_kurzweil?currentPage=all.

Bill Joy, "Why the Future Doesn't Need Us," *Wired*, April 2000.

Genesis 1:11, compiled from the New American Standard Bible, the King James Version, the American Standard Version, and the American King James Version.

Charles Darwin, *Origin of Species*, American Home Library Company, 1902, original from Harvard University, digitized November 21, 2007, http://books.google.com/books?id=QrcRAAAAYAAJ.

"The Science behind the Law," http://www.history.vt.edu/Jones/priv_hist3724/CarrieBuck/EugenicsIndex.html.

Edwin Black, "Eugenics and the Nazis—The California Connection, *San Francisco Chronicle*, November 9, 2003, http://www.sfgate.com/cgi-bin/article.cgi?f=/c/a/2003/11/09/ING9C2QSKB1.DTL&hw=edwin+black+eugenics&sn=001&sc=1000.

Charles Darwin, *The Descent of Man*, 1871, 1896, available at http://psychclassics.yorku.ca/Darwin/Descent/index.htm.

Michael Pidwirny, "Origin and Definition of Life," chapter 9 in *Fundamentals of Physical Geography*, 2nd ed., online e-book, 2006, http://www.physicalgeography.net/fundamentals/9a.html.

Edgar Allan Poe, "The Mask of the Red Death," 1842; Synopsis of film *49 Up*, dir. Michael Apted, *P.O.V.*, PBS website, October 1, 2007, http://www.pbs.org/pov/pov2007/49up/about.html.

Logan Hill, "The Tao of Christina Ricci," *New York* magazine, February 21, 2008. Excerpted with permission by *New York* magazine.

Dr. Sandra Rose Michael, "Bio-Scalar Technology," DNM, 15th Annual Area Agencies on Aging Association of Michigan Conference, 2007.

Michael McClellan, "Base 7 Numerology: Overview and FAQ," http://www .newprophecy.net/base7.htm.

"About Astrology: The Houses," iVillage website, http://www.astrology.com/ aboutastrology/interpreting/houses/house7.html.

James Burgess and Richard Grey, "7 Words: Life Management Technique," http:// www.7words.co.uk/index.php.

3hatmojo, "7 Words of Wisdom Here for You," May 13, 2009, http://3hatmojo .com/7wow/.

Jacqueline Novogratz, *The Blue Sweater*, Rodale, 2009.

Emotion Expression Humanoid Robot, Head Robot Team/Takanishi Laboratory, Humanoid Robotics Institute (HRI), Waseda University 2004–2006, http://www .takanishi.mech.waseda.ac.jp/research/we/we-3rv/index.htm.

Contactmusic.com, "Nicolas Cage—Cage's Seven-Year Tattoo Cycle," April 1, 2003, http://www.contactmusic.com/new/xmlfeed.nsf/mndwebpages/cage.s%20seven .year%20tattoo%20cycle.

Dr. Michele Borba, "7 Big Life Changes for Kids" and associated video segment on *Today* show, iVillage website, http://micheleborba.ivillage.com/parenting/archives/2008/06/7- life-changes.html.

John Emsley, "Science: The Seven Deadly Smells of a Skunk," *New Scientist*, August 4, 1990, http://www.newscientist.com/article/mg12717282.900-science-the-seven-deadly -smells-of-a-skunk-.html.

Alison George, "Seven Unsolved Medical Mysteries," *New Scientist*, December 16, 2008, http://www.newscientist.com/article/dn16273-seven-unsolved-medical-mysteries.html.

Megan Rolland and Karen Voyles, "Body in Car Identified as Gainesville Engineer," *The Gainesville Sun*, February 25, 2009, http://www.gainesville.com/article/20090225/ ARTICLES/902250971.

CHAPTER SEVEN WONDER

David Brewster, *Memoirs of the Life, Writings, and Discoveries of Sir Isaac Newton*, 1855 edition by Thomas Constable and Company, 1855, p. 331.

"Pleiades Mythology," National Astronomy and Ionosphere Center (NASA) website, pages maintained by Steven Gibson, http://www.naic.edu/~gibson/pleiades/pleiades_ myth.html, http://www.naic.edu/~gibson/pleiades/.

"Origin of the Name Subaru," Subaru Global website, 2006, http://www.subaru-global.com/origin_name.html.

"Mars Odyssey: NASA Orbiter Finds Possible Cave Skylights on Mars," NASA website, September 21, 2007, http://www.nasa.gov/mission_pages/odyssey/odyssey-20070921.html.

Steven W. Squyres, "Mars," World Book Online Reference Center, World Book, Inc., 2004, http://www.nasa.gov/worldbook/mars_worldbook.html.

Martin Rees, *Just Six Numbers*, Basic Books, 2000, pp. 2, 53.

Jennet Conant, *The Irregulars*, Simon & Schuster, 2008.

"The 40th Anniversary of the Mercury 7," NASA website, http://www.hq.nasa.gov/office/pao/History/40thmerc7/intro.htm.

Laurence R. Young bio, MIT website, http://web.mit.edu/aeroastro/www/people/lry/bio.html.

"Boeing 707," Boeing website, http://www.boeing.com/news/feature/sevenseries/707.html.

Mike Lombardi, "Why 7's Been a Lucky Number," *Boeing Frontiers*, March 2004, http://www.boeing.com/news/frontiers/archive/2004/february/i_history.html.

Alistair Weaver, "The New Porsche 911 Is Mean, Yet Green," Edmunds website, June 15, 2008, http://www.edmunds.com/insideline/do/Drives/FirstDrives/articleId=127219?tid=edmunds.il.home.photopanel..3.*.

"About ST7," NASA website, http://nmp.nasa.gov/st7/ABOUT/About_index.html.

Geoffrey Chaucer, "The Canon's Yeoman's Tale," in *The Canterbury Tales*.

"Our Seven-Day Week," http://www.webexhibits.org/calendars/week.html; "Origins of the Days of the Week," BBC website, 11 June 2002, http://www.bbc.co.uk/dna/h2g2/A698989.

"Revolutionary Calendar and Metric System," the Open University website, http://openlearn.open.ac.uk/mod/resource/view.php?id=170065.

Jayaram V, "The Symbolic Significance of Numbers in Hinduism," Hinduwebsite, http://www.hinduwebsite.com/numbers.asp.

"Seven Vows or Saptapadi," iloveindia website, http://weddings.iloveindia.com/indian-weddings/seven-vows.html.

"Transcript: Is David Koresh Jesus Christ? Waco: The Inside Story," *Frontline*, PBS website, March 17, 1993, http://www.pbs.org/wgbh/pages/frontline/waco/koreshjc.html.

D. H. Lawrence, "Seven Seals," in *New Poems*, Martin Secker, 1919, also available at Bartleby.com, http://www.bartleby.com/128/33.html.

E. W. Bullinger, *Number in Scripture*, 3rd ed. Kessinger Publishing, 2003, Google books.

Orthodox Jewish Bible, Artists for Israel International, p. 1195, available at http://www.afii.org/ojbible/1195.pdf.

Mehnaz Sahibzada, "The Symbolism of the Number Seven In Islamic Culture and Rituals," Thomson Wadsworth website, 2005, http://www.wadsworth.com/religion_d/special_features/symbols/islamic.html.

Joseph M. Champlin, "Truths Jews, Christians, and Muslims Hold in Common," *St. Anthony Messenger*, April 2002, http://www.americancatholic.org/Messenger/Apr2002/Feature2.asp.

Mark Schumacher, "Shichifukujin: Seven Lucky Gods of Japan," www.onmarkproductions.com, March 28, 2007, http://www.onmarkproductions.com/html/seven.shtml.

"The Samurai and Their Use of Bushido," Fortune City website, http://victorian.fortunecity.com/duchamp/410/bsamurai.html.

Lisa Zyga, "sQuba: World's First Underwater Car," Physorg.com website, December 20, 2007, http://www.physorg.com/news117377410.html.

"Biggest Mobile Guitar–World Record Set by Dieter Senft," World Record Academy, April 14, 2008, http://www.worldrecordsacademy.org/biggest/biggest_mobile_guitar_world_record_set_by_Dieter_Senft_80201.htm.

Jennifer Carlile, "A New Way to View London: From a Toilet," MSNBC website, March 5, 2004, http://www.msnbc.msn.com/id/4326340/.

Willy Vok, "Underwater Post Offices and Mailboxes around the World," Gadling website, April 23, 2007, http://www.gadling.com/2007/04/23/underwater-post-offices-and-mailboxes-around-the-world/.

"China Unveils First Playable Ice Piano," Wayodd website, January 15, 2008, http://www.wayodd.com/china-unveils-first-playable-ice-piano/v/8830/.

"Malawi's Football-Shaped Home," BBC website, May 8, 2006, http://news.bbc.co.uk/2/hi/africa/4946416.stm.

Paul Kelbie, "'Pavement Picasso' Dazzles Pedestrians with 3D Masterpieces," *The Independent*, August 31, 2006, http://www.independent.co.uk/news/uk/this-britain/pavement-picasso-dazzles-pedestrians-with-3d-masterpieces-414063.html.

George Miller, "The Magical Number Seven, Plus or Minus Two," *Psychological Review* 63, no. 2 (1956).

Jack Tresidder, *The Complete Dictionary of Symbols*, Chronicle Books, 2005.

"Is This Your Lucky Number?" *The Independent*, December 31, 2006, http://www
.independent.co.uk/news/uk/this-britain/is-this-your-lucky-number-seventyseven-things
-you-need-to-know-about-07-430258.html.

The Columbia Encyclopedia, 6th ed., Columbia University Press, 2001–7.

Jason M. Everett, ed., "7th Century A.D.," *The People's Chronology*, Gale Cengage, 2006,
eNotes.com website, http://www.enotes.com/peoples-chronology/year-7th-century-d.

E. Cobham Brewer, "Boots," in *Dictionary of Phrase and Fable*, Henry Altemus Company,
1898.

Associated Press, "Wisconsin Man Runs Over, Eats Seven-Legged Transgendered Deer,"
December 14, 2006, Fox News website, http://www.foxnews.com/story/
0,2933,236483,00.html.

{ CREDITS }

{ INDEX }

{ FOURTEEN FUN FACTS }

Dear Reader: Every time I thought I had exhausted all the stories and facts about the number seven, I'd discover yet another odd and interesting item, like the Seven Society Order of the Crown and Dagger, a secret organization that started at the College of William and Mary in Virginia. Many of you may also have personal stories and factual anecdotes that did not make it into this book. I'd love to read them, hear them, or even see them (if you've posted something on YouTube). So please upload your stories or factoids to my website so we can continue the conversation: www.seventhebook.com. Thank you.

Zzzzzzz

Sleep less than seven hours a night and you may be risking your life. A study by the Finnish Institute of Occupational Health determined that lack of sleep increased mortality by 26 percent in men and 21 percent in women. Less extreme, but still pretty devastating, a study in the *Journal of Clinical Sleep Medicine* claims that sleep deprivation leads to obesity. They can get you a lot of ways.

Seven Times Smarter

According to an old Chinese proverb, it is always better to think things over seven times before starting to speak. —Knowledge@Wharton

Big Boots

A European folktale features a giant who wears seven-league boots. The boots were magical and allowed the wearer to take giant strides. A league is 3 miles, so 7 leagues is 21 miles or just under 35 kilometers, both divisible by 7.

Swing Low

The seventh hole at Shinnecock Hills Golf Club is a doozy. During the 2004 U.S. Open, some of the best players struggled to make par. Phil Mickelson, a crowd favorite, barely touched his putt when the ball rolled fifteen feet past the hole. *The New York Times* said the 189-yard, par-3 challenge turned tournament play into miniature golf. Ernie Els was equally unkind in his description: "The seventh hole is unplayable," he said. "It's ridiculous." —http://tinyurl.com/pcfcxw.

The Precocious Toddler

In Hindu mythology, Buddha rose to his feet after being born and took seven steps.

Which Way Is Surrey?

London's Covent Garden has an intersection of seven roads, named Seven Dials. It's called a hidden village, where shops and restaurants flourish. But in the nineteenth century it was a Dickensian slum and had seven notorious pubs.

&

Four Tops: Just Seven Numbers

Just Seven Numbers
Can straighten out my life
But my pride won't let me phone
Just seven numbers
Can get me through to you, girl
Then I'll know you're really at home

You haven't been fair to me
Playing all that you see
You say you seen some of the act
I don't know that you're a coming back
If I only knew where you were
Just seven numbers

The Road Kill Gourmet

Wisconsin's Rick Lisko ran over a deer, which turned out to be
a hermaphrodite with seven legs. He took photos of the
creature, then turned it over to his butcher. "And by the way,
I did eat it," Lisko said. "It was tasty."

One Step at a Time

In 1963, Miles Davis recorded an
album, *Seven Steps to Heaven*.

When in Rome . . .

In France, *sept* means "seven." In Latin, *septem* is "seven."
Even though September is the ninth month of the Gregorian
calendar—the one we follow today—the month got its
name originally from the early Roman calendar.

Name Game

There's lots of discussion about which dwarf names
were rejected by Walt Disney when he made the award-winning
Snow White and the Seven Dwarfs animated film in 1937. Some of
them sound like hip hop names today, including "Biggy" and "Puffy."
A few that wouldn't make the cut in today's politically correct
world include "Tubby" and "Baldy."

Boys

Mythology surrounds the birth of a seventh son of a seventh son, who is said to possess attributes ranging from healing powers to second sight. This legend is claimed by the Irish as well as the Mohawk Indians.

❦

Girls

There are seven "Seven Sisters": the Pleiades; the Mars caves; a series of chalk cliffs on the East Sussex coast; a set of waterfalls in Norway; a group of Stalinist skyscrapers in Moscow; the original all-women top colleges (Wellesley, Bryn Mawr, Smith, Mount Holyoke, Barnard, Vassar, and Radcliffe); and the original seven sister women's magazines (*McCall's*, *Ladies' Home Journal*, *Woman's Day*, *Good Housekeeping*, *Family Circle*, *Better Homes and Gardens*, and *Redbook*).

❦

Seven Days of the Week Undies

{ ABOUT THE AUTHOR }

Media guru Jacqueline Leo has held a number of high-level positions in publishing and television. She founded and launched *Child* magazine in 1986, and went on to be editor in chief of *Family Circle* magazine and editorial director of the New York Times Women's Magazine Group, where she launched *Fitness* magazine. She was senior producer and editorial director of ABC's *Good Morning America*; editorial director for *Consumer Reports* magazine; and vice president and editor in chief of *Reader's Digest*. She is currently director of digital operations for the Peter G. Peterson Foundation. She lives in New York City.

{ ABOUT TWELVE }

TWELVE

TWELVE was established in August 2005 with the objective of publishing no more than one book per month. We strive to publish the singular book, by authors who have a unique perspective and compelling authority. Works that explain our culture; that illuminate, inspire, provoke, and entertain. We seek to establish communities of conversation surrounding our books. Talented authors deserve attention not only from publishers, but from readers as well. To sell the book is only the beginning of our mission. To build avid audiences of readers who are enriched by these works—that is our ultimate purpose.